And...So We Walked

The Inspirational Story of a Couple's Walk Across America

Rick and Jane McKinney

© Rick and Jane McKinney 2023

rickandjanemckinney@gmail.com, https://andsowewalked.org
(815)662-8144

TABLE OF CONTENTS

INTRODUCTION 1

PROLOGUE 2

CHAPTER 1 4

CHAPTER 2 8

CHAPTER 3 12

CHAPTER 4 21

CHAPTER 5 28

CHAPTER 6 38

CHAPTER 7 47

CHAPTER 8 52

CHAPTER 9 59

CHAPTER 10 67

CHAPTER 11 74

CHAPTER 12 85

CHAPTER 13 91

CHAPTER 14 96

CHAPTER 15 101

CHAPTER 16 109

CHAPTER 17	115
CHAPTER 18	120
CHAPTER 19	127
CHAPTER 20	136
CHAPTER 21	141
CHAPTER 22	147
CHAPTER 23	153
CHAPTER 24	162
CHAPTER 25	169
CHAPTER 26	174
CHAPTER 27	180
CHAPTER 28	189
CHAPTER 29	194
CHAPTER 30	202
CHAPTER 31	208
CHAPTER 32	213
CHAPTER 33	216
CHAPTER 34	223
ONE FINAL THOUGHT AND CHALLENGE	226
APPENDIX ONE	228

Introduction

This is an extraordinary story. It also happens to be true. As you read the following pages, you may wonder if some exaggeration has made its way into the narrative. I can assure you that what you are about to read is an honest and accurate account of our journey. That will, however, make it no less unbelievable.

There have been many people who have attempted cross-country treks and failed. We should have been two of those people. There was no reason to believe we could successfully walk from one side of the country to the other except one; we had been called to do it by the God of the impossible. It was the hardest challenge of our lives, bar none. It was also the most amazing experience two people could have.

As you read, you may be surprised by the amount of detail with which the story is told. This was made possible by the relentless journaling and record-keeping of my wife, best friend, lifelong partner and fellow walker, Jane. Every mile was documented, landmarks were noted and the name of every person we met along the way was written down. In addition, the walk was corroborated with photographs, newspaper and television coverage, radio interviews, Internet blogs and personal appearances.

We hope reading this book will inspire you to answer God's call in your life. No matter who you are or your life circumstances, He has a plan and purpose for you to fulfill. May the pages ahead bring a new dedication to walk where God leads you.

Rick and Jane McKinney

PROLOGUE

The emergency room was complete with bright lights, doctors and nurses in scrubs and stainless-steel trays with long hypodermic needles. Some of the medical staff were poking and prodding their way around in examination while others rolled their portable machines in and out of the cramped room. It was remarkably like a scene on television. The weeping wife was the most difficult thing to see, worried more than anyone would ever know about the patient who lay on the emergency room stretcher. Watching her brought tears to the husband's eyes as he struggled to reassure her by clenching her hand in his.

What made this scene different from any I'd seen before, even when I had been summoned to emergency rooms as a pastor, was seeing it all happen from the patient's perspective. It was all happening to me. The patient they were examining was me. The hospital wristband had my name on it and this time, my wife was standing there.

I could hear the emergency room doctor carrying on a phone conversation with the Burn Center at the desk just across the hall from my room. He was talking about me. Fighting back the urge to close my eyes and sleep, I strained to hear what he was saying but could only catch a few words here and there. Now a different doctor, an orthopedic surgeon, had entered the overcrowded quarters and was pulling and tugging on my left index finger. Although he was pulling hard enough to make him grimace, the Lidocaine, administered in five or six shots had done its job and I could only feel some slight pressure.

Ever since I was hospitalized at age seven to have my tonsils removed, I had never been able to smell the distinct mixture of hospital aromas without feeling nauseated. I couldn't tell if the smell, the drugs, or the trauma caused me to feel as though I might pass out, but I struggled to stay awake.

The emergency room doctor was off the phone now and a conference was happening in the hall just outside my room. They broke their huddle and came alongside my temporary bed. "Mr. McKinney, I just got off the phone with the Burn Center in Little Rock and we've decided the best thing is to go ahead and transfer you there right now," the man in the white coat and stethoscope said with no emotion. It was the last thing I wanted to hear, but before it could sink in the orthopedic surgeon took his turn. "I was able to put your dislocated finger back into place, but I'm not sure what kind of function you will have. It was a severe injury. There is a good chance you will need surgery to repair it later, but your burns are the primary concern right now. We will put your finger in a splint and give you some instructions for taking care of it. Before we transfer you, do you have any questions?"

Did I have any questions? Only a couple of dozen like, "How long will I be off my feet?" or "Will this stop our walk across America?" or "Did I hear something about skin grafts?" or "Will I ever be able to play the piano again?" But as those questions were racing through my mind, only one was critical. Only one question was going to make any real difference. Only one question would come out of my mouth. I looked as intently as I could at the doctor and tried to shake off the effects of the morphine. "Just one," I said, "just one…."

Chapter 1

(18 months earlier)

The voice was as clear as I'd ever heard.

"Do you believe it?"

I thought perhaps someone had slipped in behind me and seen me reading my Bible.

"Do you believe it?"

This time I turned to see who was questioning my faith in God's Word. No one was there. I reread it. Joshua chapter 1 verse 3, "Every place on which the sole of your foot treads, I have given it to you...."

Again, the question, *"Do you believe it?"*

This was one of my favorite passages of Scripture. I had read Joshua chapter 1 many times. The first few pages of Joshua in my Bibles were all heavily marked with sermon notes, mine and others. That made the repeated question even more annoying. Of course, I believed it. Without thinking, I said out loud, "Yes, I believe!"

Now the question changed. *"What do you believe?"*

I now realized the voice I heard was not human; it wasn't coming from inside the room. It was coming from within my spirit. That, however, did not make it any less real.

"I believe You said that to Joshua," I replied.

"But do you believe it?" the Voice asked.

I questioned, "Do I believe it for me?" wanting to understand what He was after.

"Yes. Do you believe the promise is for you? Do you believe the principle?"

"The principle?"

"Yes. The principle. That you can take possession of the land by walking through it."

"I'm not sure; I've never thought about it."

"The principle has always been true. Where Adam walked was his. Where Abraham walked was his. When the children of Israel walked around Jericho, it became theirs. It's always been true."

"What does that have to do with me? Where do I need to walk?"

"What do you want to claim?"

"America. My country."

"Then walk it."

"All of it?"

"Whatever you want to claim."

"I want it all. But not for myself. I want it for You."

"Then walk it all in My Name."

It wasn't rational. It wasn't something I wanted to do. I could think of a thousand reasons not even to entertain the thought, not the least of which was that I was anything but an athlete. What about money? What about our ministry? Oh no! What about my wife?

She had seen me through every idea, goal, dream and vision for 30 years. She had stood by my side when everyone else had written me off. She was seldom surprised when I started a sentence with, "I think God is speaking to me about ..." But walking across America? I was sure this was where she would draw the line.

And so, I kept silent about the conversation between God and me. Days turned into weeks. I had never kept anything from Jane this long. It wouldn't go away. I was more and more obsessed with it. Already I was planning. How could it work? I had secretly looked at a map. I calculated the mileage. The shortest route quickly figured, was almost 3000 miles! What could I walk in a day? How many days? Is it even possible?

Finally, I couldn't hide what had become my enthusiasm for the walk any longer. She was going to see it in my eyes soon anyway. She could always tell when God and I were scheming. If I didn't initiate the conversation soon, she would. Then I might not be prepared. I had to get ready to tell her. I had to make it seem possible. But how do you make walking across America, for what I now estimated would be nearly half a year, seem feasible?

I want to pause here to share a great spiritual and practical truth that could easily be lost in the storyline. There is absolutely no substitute for having a spouse and life partner who is also a spiritual partner and sojourner. I do not mean, as some may assume, that you must have a partner who is a "yes person." I'm not talking about someone who is weak and subservient and who goes along with any hair-brained idea that pops into your mind. No, that is definitely not Jane. As I was soon to learn on a deeper level than ever before, she is the strongest person physically, spiritually, emotionally, and mentally I have ever known. I would learn more of her fortitude and faith in six months than I had in our relationship of over a third of a century. She lovingly challenges me and makes me examine my claims. She talks me through my sometimes-faulty logic and gently guides me to a saner place. Taking a new idea to her is a little scary but also exciting because I know what emerges from our conversations will be much closer to the truth. After all, she has been a part of the process. Having a person in your life who makes you better and sharper than you'd be alone is part of God's intent for most of us. When we miss that, we miss a huge advantage which is a part of His desire for our lives.

And so, you can understand the mixed emotions with which I timidly approached the subject of walking across America. I started to broach the subject several times, but just getting prepared to tell her made the whole thing seem so ridiculous. How could I ever defend this plan to her? And how would I get anyone else to believe it if I couldn't defend it to her? That was it. I knew I had to tell her. I now believed it with all my heart. Telling her would be the first test. I had to see if I could convince others to believe it too.

Chapter 2

Jane certainly struggled with the suggestion of walking across America. "Can't we just ride bikes?" was her first response. When I explained that the soles of our feet were part of the principle, she understood why we couldn't. But her next question was the most critical. "Why do it at all?"

As it turned out, I hadn't anticipated this question. Jane was the first, but she would certainly not be the last to ask the obvious: Why walk across America?

I never asked why because as soon as God reminded me of the principle, I knew why. You see, God had invested several years preparing my heart and convicting my spirit about how our nation had begun slipping away from Him. As a matter of fact, I had been sharing this conviction all year as we traveled the country. I knew our nation was in desperate need of repentance. Our nation needed reclaiming. When I say nation, I am not talking simply about just the usual targets. God was burdening my heart for our entire country, from top to bottom and left to right. We needed healing from angry words and loveless religion. We needed something more than empty words about heaven and hell. We needed a revival of Jesus-ism, plain and simple.

Jane accepted the call more quickly than I did. She had heard those sermons and I had shared my convictions with her as I studied. She knew the need for spiritual renewal in America. As an avid reader, she had read numerous accounts of the great spiritual awakenings that swept America early in its history. Those years of increased awareness of God's presence were not about people being driven to one side of the political spectrum or the other. The real impact of the outpouring of God's Spirit was that people were driven to their knees. We both longed for a day when God's conviction would again fall on our nation. I'm sure she had her internal battles. But in her heart, she knew God was speaking and calling us to put the soles of our feet down across this land and claim it, reclaim it, for His Kingdom.

I don't think there was a specific moment when we both looked at each other and said, "Let's do it." As soon as we understood the spiritual principle, we were willing to step into that principle literally. We knew in our hearts that we would walk. At least we would begin to *plan* to walk across America.

I am a dreamer. I am a planner, a visionary, and a certified "head in the clouds" creative soul. I have always been a daydreamer. My mother worried about me as an adolescent because I could sit alone for hours and "think." I wasn't thinking about math equations or where to go to college. I fantasized about how things could be, might be, and should be someday. I was "imagining" with John Lennon, going to the "mountaintop" with Martin Luther King Jr. and envisioning "the new frontier" with JFK. I have dreamed a million dreams that have never made it further than the space between my ears. For all the optimism a dreamer like me expresses, there is always a certain amount of skepticism because so many dreams have failed to materialize.

So, it was with the dream of walking across America. At this point, it was a dream. A noble goal, to be sure. It was a dream with an important spiritual principle behind it, without a doubt. It was a dream that could potentially be a part of a fresh move of God across this nation! But it was, at least at this point, only a dream. Because it was a dream, there was a chance it would not happen. I'm unsure how to explain it, but somehow, I was compelled to make this dream come true. I could not allow it to die on the drawing board of my soul.

Whatever it took, if it cost me everything I had, Jane and I needed to walk together across America.

There was but one way, humanly speaking, this dream could become a reality; lots and lots of planning, hard work and preparation. I was not ruling out God's supernatural provision and ability to accomplish the task, but I was unwilling to sit back and wait for Him to make it happen.

Jane and I began to pour over maps. Picking the route, at least the general path we would take, was easy. We started calculating idealistically, with no practical experience in walking, to figure out how long it would take. We sat around the table night after night planning. There were nights when I would look up from the maps or the "to-do" lists and see Jane had fallen asleep with her head on the table.

We started to walk regularly. At first, we walked a couple of miles per day. We visited pro shops and shoe stores to get advice. We learned more about feet, shoes, and socks than we ever wanted to know. I started scouring the Internet to see if anyone else had done what we were planning to do. We began to work into our conversations with trusted friends that we were going to walk across America. We went to talk with our Pastor to share our plan with him. He didn't even flinch. We shared it with my godly parents, and even though they had seen so many of my dreams fail, they never said a negative word. They supported our vision of walking across America as fully as if God had also spoken to them, and who knows, maybe He had. Then, one by one, we started sharing with an ever-increasing circle of friends, family, and supporters that we were planning the adventure of a lifetime, a walk across America. We were now obligated and committed to God and the people whose opinions and approval mattered to us. We had passed the point of no return. We could not turn back now.

Each day we walked further and longer and pushed our bodies and our limits. We talked with someone who had just completed a cross-country walk and made careful notes of his advice. Every bit of information was valuable; what kind of rain gear to purchase, what kind of weather we could expect and even how to deal with inevitable issues like going to the bathroom. Catalogs from Bass Pro® and Cabela's® became our everyday reading material. We scheduled planning meetings with a close circle of friends in the ministry and began praying earnestly that God would help us know how to plan, raise needed funds and recruit a support team, both on the road and back home.

We became obsessed with preparation. We began to purchase a few things here and there as we could afford them. We walked. The brochures were printed, a website was created, a special email address and a toll-free phone number were secured. We walked. All our contacts, personal and ministry-related, were asked to help support our walk. We walked. Everywhere we went, we talked about the *Walk to Reclaim America* with increasing confidence. We walked. A few folks were beginning to believe. Then a few more. Finally, we were just a few weeks away. We held one giant rally at our home church to explain the vision one last time, received financial gifts and pledges for the walk and then it was time to leave for California, the starting point for the walk.

The *Walk to Reclaim America* was going to happen; at least it was going to begin. We would have to walk more than twice as far each day than we had ever walked thus far, day after day after day. But we were as ready as we could get. The time for talking and planning was over. It was time to go. We walked to the vehicle, pointed it due west, and we were off.

Chapter 3

It was almost impossible to believe. Everything had that fuzzy look to it, you know, slightly out of focus. Part of it was the overcast skies and the mist in the air. But there was also a surreal feeling at that moment. It was almost as though I was watching from outside myself as we walked up Santa Monica Pier to the designated starting place.

It was January 1st, 2006. Finally. We had anticipated this day for fifteen months. We had prepared our bodies, or at least we thought we had. We had walked over 1500 miles in the preceding 12 months. We had planned and driven the routes. We had spent untold hours preparing for this moment. We were beginning the most daring adventure and the most physically challenging event of our lives, already mentally, emotionally, and physically exhausted. We had taken no time off to rest for over a year, choosing instead to use every spare moment to train, have garage and yard sales, visit with supporters, move out of our home, put it up for sale and of course, maintain a full ministry schedule every weekend.

So, this was it. We were standing on Santa Monica pier, exactly where Forrest Gump had gone before us, getting ready to begin what would turn out to be a turning point in both of our lives. We were literally stepping into the unknown. No amount of preparation could have gotten us ready for what we were about to attempt. Our only hope, it would turn out, was the One who had called us to this enormous task in the first place.

God used a wide variety of means to encourage us, support us, and guide us through many difficult times and places. One of the most important was through the love and support of friends and family. That first day was no exception. I know now that Jane and I would have begun the walk that morning even if no one had shown up to see us off, but I'm glad it wasn't like that. We were surrounded, not by hundreds of cheering supporters as I had allowed myself to imagine more than a few times during the months leading up to this day. Instead, there were nine; our two drivers for the month of January, a family of four from Rogers, Arkansas, and two people from our home church, Levi and Pastor Mark. Each was important in their own way and represented different areas of our lives and ministry, but there is no doubt the strongest supporter present was our Pastor.

Having grown up in a pastor's home and then having pastored myself for some twenty years, I had little experience in how much the support of a pastor, who's not your dad, could mean. That Sunday morning as our pastor knelt with us on Santa Monica Pier and prayed

God's blessing on the walk, it meant more to us than it is possible to convey. Pastor Mark prayed, made a few brief comments and then our first steps were simulcast back to our home church in Harrison, Ohio. Just to know our pastor had led our church to be a faithful support team for the *Walk to Reclaim America* was just unbelievable. I cannot imagine even starting a spiritual venture like this one without the wholehearted support and complete commitment of our pastor.

Pastor Mark was the last to wave goodbye as we took those first steps by ourselves down the sidewalk toward the first turn. We were taking our first steps on Route 66. The old "mother road," where it still existed, would be our home for the next 1400 miles. Jane and I held hands for a few moments and then both realized we couldn't keep the pace our feet had memorized over the last year while holding hands. As we rounded the first turn of our journey, right on Santa Monica Boulevard, the sights and sounds of the streets, surprisingly busy so early on a Sunday morning in Los Angeles, all seemed to be magnified and intensified. During the next nine hours, we saw and experienced a colorful cross-section of America. Few other cities could have offered such a collage. In our first few blocks, we met and talked with many who were homeless. A few hours later we walked awestruck through the opulence of Beverly Hills. We observed so many different ethnic and culturally diverse neighborhoods, it was like taking a quick trip around the world. There were skin colors in every shade imaginable. There were foreign languages and dialects of English so varied it left our ears tingling. We passed through thickly populated areas where people were beginning to cook, and restaurants were preparing their first meals of the day. The air was filled with the pungent smells of spices and mysterious ingredients. Some people passed us trance-like. Others were curious about why two white people, dressed alike in red, white, and blue would be walking through their part of town. Most did not smile back, and few responded to our greetings with much more than a grunt. We became the minority in more ways than one that day; sometimes because of our skin color, sometimes because of our faith, and sometimes because of our sexual orientation. During the first day of the walk across America, I cannot imagine a kind of person we did not encounter. What a blessing it was to have been able to preview our country to such a degree on the very first day of the walk.

At the end of our first day, we had walked 21 miles, more than twice as far as we had ever walked in a single day. Even still, we were almost a mile from our planned stopping point. We were so tired and our feet so sore we could not imagine walking another step…not tomorrow, not ever. I wondered if I had just made the biggest blunder of my life. And to top it off, we had walked the last half of the day in light to moderate rain with a forecast for more rain the next day.

More rain was exactly what we got. It had rained all night and was raining when we began walking on Monday morning. We were planning to walk down Colorado Boulevard through Pasadena, California on January 2nd, the day after the Rose Bowl Parade. At least we thought it was the day after. What Southern Californians know that we didn't is that when January 1st falls on Sunday the big parade is held on Monday. So here we were on the second day of the walk, sore and tired from the longest walk of our lives on Sunday, facing hard-driving rain, and trudging through tens of thousands of people along the parade route. Did I say we were ecstatic? Well, we were. We'd watched the Rose Bowl Parade on television all our lives and always wished we could be there. After less than an hour of walking, we turned a corner and found ourselves right in the middle of the parade, right in front of the television cameras, just as the Disney float passed and began shooting off fireworks. We were close enough to see the princesses' smiles and smell the gunpowder of the fireworks. It was as though God had arranged the whole thing and was saying, "You're on the right track. This one's for you!"

Strangely, we didn't feel like we were on the right track. We were only a little over a day into the walk and we were already off the path we had laid out. We weren't really sure where we were, compared to where we were supposed to be. We did know we weren't where we had planned on walking. Worse than the drenching rain, which had already soaked our socks and clothes through our Gortex® rain gear and having to wind our way through the crowds, was that the parade route was blocked, and our driver had gone on ahead…way ahead. Actually, he'd gotten so far ahead that our walkie-talkies couldn't reach him and we had no idea where he was. Our primitive (by today's standards) flip phones had gotten drenched by the rain and were ruined. We walked for what seemed like a hundred miles before we found him parked around a corner, thirteen miles from our starting point. It was already way past lunchtime, we were wringing wet, and much to our dismay, we hadn't brought nearly enough dry socks. When I took off my shoes and socks at lunch, I could see huge blisters forming on my feet from walking in water-logged socks. I tried to dry the socks during lunch with the heater in the van to no avail. When lunch was over, we put our wet socks and shoes back on and stepped back out into the rain which was still coming down in sheets. We had long since stopped trying to avoid the puddles and flooded gutters. The goal now was just to keep walking long enough to get in our twenty miles.

We did learn an important lesson during day two of the walk while trying to navigate through what was literally the largest group of people we'd ever seen. You simply can't talk to everyone you see. We determined that we had three main purposes in walking across America. One was to intercede or pray for America and its people. The second was to encourage other believers to share their faith, become involved in their communities and let their voices be heard in matters of conscience and faith. The third, and this very quickly became the central theme of the walk, was to encounter people one on one with the love, joy, and good news of the gospel. This third purpose necessarily involved talking with people face to face. Our first tendency was to want to talk to everyone. The more we talked to people about Jesus and His incredible love, the more we wanted to talk. It doesn't take a genius to figure out that if you spend all your time talking, you're not going to get much walking done. It was to become one of the toughest balancing acts of the next six months. We *were* on a timetable, one which we believed God had helped us map out.

On the other hand, there were people all around us who needed to hear what was on our hearts, and most importantly, on God's heart. We had been called to share a message of reconciliation and peace, not condemnation and judgment. Almost immediately, we began to make choices about which people to begin conversations with and which ones to simply pass by with a smile or a nod. Our prayer was that those decisions were made in response to the Spirit's leadership,

I must admit we almost missed an opportunity on day two because of me. By mid-afternoon, I was beginning to feel the blisters on my feet. The rain had beaten me down a little and I was ready for day two to be over. There was a very short period where the rain stopped, and the clouds parted. We were in Arcadia, California. I thought this was a great opportunity to make up for some lost time. We could take our rain hoods down for a while and maybe just dry out as we walked. Honestly, I wasn't looking for anyone to talk to. I just wanted to walk.

As we made our way down Foothills Boulevard, a man in a camouflage jacket crossed the street toward us. We were just a bit ahead of him and so he crossed just a little behind us. I thought I heard him call out to us, but I wasn't sure, so I just kept walking. He called again, this time a little louder, and so we stopped and turned around.

"Hey, ya got a dollar?" the man asked.

"Why do ya need a dollar?" I asked back.

"I need to buy some milk," was his quick comeback.

OK. So, we're drenched. It's getting late. I'm hurting and here's a guy whom I'm pretty sure, based on lots of experience, isn't really interested in buying milk. He doesn't smell like alcohol, but he's shaking like he needs a drink.

Being the evangelistic and spiritually minded person I am, my first thought was to give the guy a dollar and get on our way. Oh sure, I would have said, "God bless you" or something spiritual, but really, I just wanted to get off my feet. I began to fumble around in my waist pack for a dollar bill while Jane kept talking.

Jane had set her course in a different direction and this wouldn't be the last time her spiritual maturity would put mine to shame. The request for a dollar didn't sidetrack her, or maybe she just heard him wrong, but she just started asking this man about his relationship with God and whether he knew Jesus. I'm standing there like a dummy, watching Jane interact with this guy in a way and on a level I'd never seen her do before. I was proud of her and ashamed of myself all in an instant. I shook off the effects of the shock just as this man, who we now knew as Anthony, was answering Jane's question about knowing Jesus.

"No, I don't…but I sure would like to."

I joined the conversation as we led Anthony through the essence of what it meant to have a relationship with the Heavenly Father. He had heard The Story before. Others before us had sprinkled some of the "precious seed" into Anthony's life. Perhaps someone had shown him God's love in ways that watered and cultivated the good news sown into the good soil of his heart. But God had arranged for Jane and me to be present at harvest time. For reasons only God knows, He blessed us with the amazing privilege of leading Anthony to a tearful embrace of the

Savior, to pray and ask forgiveness for his sin and to make a life choice to serve and follow Him.

Street evangelism can sometimes leave a new convert with little hope of discipleship and the kind of meaningful connection to the family of God which will help them become grounded in their faith. We tried to begin that process with Anthony. We spent quite a bit of time going over what had just happened. His background made him reluctant to accept the fact God had completely forgiven him. We tried to give him that assurance. It was also difficult for him to believe he would spend eternity in heaven based on what had just happened. Jane worked especially hard on this point; trying to impress on Anthony it was because of God's mercy and not his behavior we would see him in heaven someday. Lastly, we made sure Anthony knew where there was a local church; a community of believers he could adopt as his own. He said he did. We encouraged him to go as soon as possible, share with the pastor what he had done, make a public declaration of his new-found faith in Christ, and be baptized. We also encouraged him to begin telling others what he had done.

I understand this was not the perfect situation. The pastor in me wanted to stick around a few days and take care of this guy. But remember, we didn't go out looking for Anthony. I was, at best, a reluctant evangelist. Anthony called out to us, in more ways than one. Perhaps others, who could have formed long-term relationships with him, had been given countless opportunities to lead Anthony to the Lord and had not been obedient to the call. I don't know about any of that, but I do know three things. One, we were allowed to share the gospel with Anthony. Two, without any pressure he joyfully received the offer of salvation. Three, there was immediate evidence something had changed in Anthony's heart.

Do you remember why Anthony stopped us in the first place? He needed a dollar for "milk". Through the early part of Jane's conversation with him, I had located a single dollar bill and held it in my hand the whole time. As we were getting ready to leave, I offered Anthony the dollar. He wouldn't take it. He shook his head and refused it saying he no longer needed it.

We knew what Anthony was probably planning to do with that dollar. After his encounter with Christ, he couldn't take the dollar under false pretenses. He simply couldn't do it. There had been a change in his heart.

As we walked away from Anthony, with tears in our own eyes, we both agreed that if Anthony was the only reason for the *Walk to Reclaim America,* he was enough of a reason. We would not have to walk far to know Anthony was only the beginning. And…so we walked.

Chapter 4

During the remainder of our first week, we would come to understand that the walk was about many things, about so many kinds of encounters, and about so many personal lessons Jane and I needed to learn. Anthony would have been enough, but there was so much more.

For example, we learned the first week about bus stops. Many folks think if you want to touch people's lives with the gospel, you need to go to a raunchy brothel or tavern, or maybe a place of hopelessness like an inner-city homeless shelter. I suggest you start at the nearest bus stop. Just spend a couple of hours sitting there talking to the people God brings your way. Honestly, we found more hurting people ready to hear the gospel at bus stops than any other single place across America. It all started with Alice. She was sitting at a bus stop just around the corner from Anthony. We almost passed her by but then went back. As we shared with her and told her what we were doing, she began to cry. We asked if we could pray with her about anything and she just opened up to us about her family and her sons. They had drifted far from God and needed prayer. We bowed right there at the bus stop and prayed for Alice and her family. We even prayed right through her bus coming, but she caught the next one and didn't seem to mind.

During the first week, we also learned to watch for other believers who needed to be encouraged and congratulated for taking a stand. In Upland, California we saw a tire store with a nicely painted sign quoting John 3:16 on the front of their business. We crossed the six lanes of traffic and went in just to say hello. There we met Bill and Eva Espinoza, vibrant Christians, who had been threatened by city officials to take the scripture down. Bill had stood his ground, and as a result, there is a constant reminder to the thousands who pass by his shop every day that God loves them. We prayed with them too, asking God to bless their tire business.

On day four we learned God would always give us the strength to overcome whatever obstacles seemed to be in our way. It was the end of our day, and we were leaving the city. We had four miles yet to walk and when we turned north toward the mountains, we began to be blasted by the Santa Ana winds. They were, without a doubt, the strongest winds we had ever tried to walk in. We would learn later that those winds were 55 – 60 m.p.h. As we trudged through Fontana, California, the winds were so strong we had to lean over at what seemed like nearly a 45-degree angle just to hold our own against the wind. As we got out to the edge of town where there was nothing but sand, we started to get pelted, almost sandblasted, by the blowing granules. Jane begged me to have our driver pick us up, take us to the end of the four miles and then walk the route with our backs to the wind. I wanted to say yes because she was having such a hard time walking, but I just had a check in my spirit about it. I really felt there was something to learn by going forward. For the last mile or two, we were in a construction zone. There was no shoulder to walk on. We were walking off the side of the road in rough, sharp gravel. When the construction equipment and trucks would pass us, they would throw up small gravel and stones and hit us in the face. When a truck was coming, I'd wrap my arms around Jane and protect her from the spray. It has become one of my fondest memories of the entire walk. It was one of the few times in all our years together that I felt my presence was able to shelter and protect her. She had always been the braver of us, but on this day, I felt like the hero.

As we walked into that horrendous wind, I heard Jane singing. I think at first it was to keep from yelling at me, but she was singing. I joined her. Then I started singing a song and even clapping. Soon we were both singing and clapping and praising God during the howling wind and sandstorm. I really sensed we needed to walk forward. The spiritual lesson for the day was that when things get rough, we can't just turn around and head in the other direction. It seemed to me that if God could get us through this, He could get us through anything.

And He was faithful. It took nearly two hours, but we walked the last four miles of the day. We even got to share Christ with some construction workers along the way. But here's the most amazing part of the story. For several days we'd seen "USA" spray-painted on the street. It was always accompanied by an arrow that pointed in the direction we were going. We thought it was pretty neat since we were walking across the USA in that direction. But when we got to the end of our four miles that windy, sandy day, Jane looked down and saw the most amazing thing. There on the street were spray-painted these words: "USA McKinney" and then an arrow in the new direction we would be taking the next day. God had just shown us if we would just walk; faithfully, and obediently walk where He led, He would never leave us, always empower us, and confirm His presence and guidance in our lives unmistakably.

By the way, that new direction turned out to be straight up a mountain over El Cajon Pass. The problem was, except for the Interstate, which we could not get permission to walk on in California, there was no other road over the mountain. As we headed into day six it looked like we were stuck. We had anticipated this problem to some extent and thought we had some alternative roads planned. But when it came right down to it, those changes were going to mean several extra days of walking on some very treacherous roads in a remote part of the desert.

At the end of day five, we walked to the end of Route 66 before we were to head over the mountain. As we were getting ready to pack up and head back to camp for the evening, we spotted a County Sheriff. We asked him for his ideas, but he had no suggestions. About that time a Fire Ranger drove up. We explained our problem, and he gave us specific directions for how to get through this portion of the desert and back to Route 66.

The next morning, we took the Ranger's route, but the road ran into a deep ravine. So now we were on our own. This section was one of the few places where we simply had no idea what to do or where to go. We had to go north toward Victorville, but that was about all we knew. There were simply no roads, so we took off through the desert. The first obstacle, and I know this sounds strange in the desert, was a quickly rising stream. The warm temperatures were causing melting snow from the mountains to run into this stream. We needed to avoid getting our feet wet first thing in the morning. My blisters were horrible by this point, and I just couldn't imagine walking all day with wet feet again. I tried to gather some large stones and make a walkway across the stream. In doing so, I dropped the walkie-talkie into the ice-cold water. So much for communicating with the driver. He now had no idea where we were going or where to meet us later. I finally got across the stream myself, but the stream was quite a bit higher by the time I did. Jane couldn't cross. I threw a rock in to try and make a "bridge," but by the time I got back with another one, the one I had just thrown in would be covered with rushing water. She finally had to just jump from rock to rock across the stream. I caught her hand on the last jump and pulled her over to the other side. In retrospect, it certainly wasn't the toughest obstacle we would face, but at the time I felt confident, actually a little like Superman, having conquered the stream. Throughout the walk, these kinds of experiences would often be preceded by a direct word from Scripture that prepared us for the event. That morning Jane had read these words to me from her Bible: "When you pass through the waters, I will be with you. When you pass through the rivers, they will not sweep over you…" (Isaiah 43:2). She thought it odd that morning because we planned to be walking through the desert all day. Little did she know, God already knew exactly where we would be walking and that in the middle of that desert, there would be a rising stream.

Up through the bluffs following the railroad tracks we went. At the top of the mesa, there were three separate train tracks. We met a photographer there who was taking pictures of the trains with the mountains as a backdrop. He warned us about rattlesnakes on warm days like this one. We kept walking, just kind of "feeling our way" through the desert, trying to find landmarks and walk toward them. It took us half of the morning to cover a distance that would have taken less than an hour on the Interstate. We did find our driver at the next exit but were still several miles short of Route 66. After looking without success for another desert road to take. We finally found a fire station where the Ranger on duty gave us a map of the "fire roads" through the desert.

Over the next few hours, I experienced several more circumstances that would end in a set of victories. First, we would have to walk through the desert where there were no roads and the possibility of getting lost was real. Second, there would be the likelihood of wild animals, snakes, scorpions or stray dogs (one of my biggest concerns). Third, we would be walking through some very narrow passes that we would have to share with trains. Fourth, since my walkie-talkie was dead, we would be entirely without communication if we needed help. Last, I was walking on nothing but blisters, and quite frankly, I had never walked in such pain.

As it happened, we did get slightly lost a couple of times. We encountered stray dogs. We did walk through a pass at the same time as a train and were so close we could have touched it. We climbed El Cajon, a sandy, vertical ascent of nearly 4000 feet from where we had begun the morning. Through it all God was faithful. Jane and I decided to have a Bible study as we walked. It was one we referred to time and time again throughout the walk. Even here on the back roads of the desert, God continued to give us people to talk to, share our faith with, and encourage in their faith walk. For example, we met a father and his sons riding their ATVs, only one of the countless opportunities God would give us in places where the difficult, "less-traveled" road gave us exposure to people whom we would otherwise have missed.

The first week ended on the outskirts of Victorville, California. It had been, in many ways, the longest seven days of our lives. And it had certainly been one we'd never forget. It had drawn me closer to the Lord and closer to my wife than I had ever been to either. I had experienced pain and victory like never in my life. Honestly, I could not imagine how I could do this for twenty-five more weeks. I also could not imagine how I could not do this for the rest of my life. And…so we walked.

Chapter 5

I could characterize each week of the walk by simply saying "ditto". Each week we saw the hand of God move in very distinct ways. Each week He provided for our needs, gave us opportunities to share with and encourage others and drew us closer to Himself. So, in those ways, every week was similar.

What makes the story of the walk across America so moving though, is how He continued to do it in new and unique ways every day, day after day. Week two was no exception as God moved in mysterious, quirky, out-of-the-ordinary and even miraculous ways, to accomplish His purpose in our lives and in the lives of others.

By the time we got to the north side of Victorville, it was lunchtime. We saw a man walking toward us on the small, sandy shoulder of the road. This was a little unusual because we encountered very few people walking once we got out of the cities. The man walking toward us was a tall, broad-shouldered, smiling, African American man. I hated to be prejudiced, but when I saw a man walking in the California heat instead of driving, and he was SMILING, I just knew he had to know Jesus. When he was close enough, I reached out my hand and introduced myself and Jane to Charles. I was right. He was a believer. He was excited about our walk across America and after we shared with Charles for a while, we asked if we could have prayer with him. He enthusiastically agreed, so we held hands in a circle and I prayed. During the prayer, I said something about all of us being called, and how we should all answer God's call on our lives.

When I finished, Charles looked up with tears in his eyes and said, "How did you know?"

"How did I know what?" I said.

"How did you know I'm called? God has called me to preach, to start a church, but I've been afraid," Charles confessed. "But I'm going to go home and tell my wife that if you two can walk across America, we can start our church!" I have often wondered about the church Charles started and how many people have found Jesus because he encountered two crazy, obedient followers of Christ along the side of the road.

The old road from Victorville to Barstow, California is still intact and still retains many of the old landmarks. Many of the little gas stations and tourist attractions are closed now, but most are still recognizable. One of the quirky sights along this part of the "mother-road" was a "bottle-tree" farm. There were hundreds of "trees" made of metal poles with little metal or wood "branches". Each of these branches had a different type of bottle on it. It was just one of those sights that made us wonder and then smile.

It was along this old stretch of Route 66 we met Mike, the truck driver. As we walked along the road, we spotted a Werner semi pulling off onto the shoulder just ahead of us. We happened to know a driver for Werner in Oklahoma City and we thought, "No, it can't be him way out here in California, can it?" It wasn't him. It was a driver named Mike, and he was lost. I thought professional truck drivers never got lost. Perhaps I shouldn't have, but I mentioned that to Mike. He assured me that he really was lost and wanted to know if we could help. We didn't have any maps with us, but we radioed our driver to bring a map for him. In the meantime, we talked to Mike about the Lord and his relationship with Him. Mike said he was a Christian but had kind of "slipped away" from God. He said he knew he needed to be closer to the Lord and so we said we'd be praying for him.

After we got Mike the directions, things got a little complicated. Mike needed to go in the opposite direction and was going to have to do a U-turn. He wanted to know if we could help by holding back traffic in both directions long enough for him to get turned around. I wasn't excited about it because of the safety factor. I guess I didn't mind too much for me, but I didn't want Jane trying to hold back traffic. Anyway, we reluctantly said we'd do it. Jane was always up for an adventure. Me, not so much.

It was probably a sight to behold. Here we were, in the hot California desert, dressed alike, holding back all the traffic on Route 66, just so Mike could turn his semi around. He did, and he waved goodbye as he drove off. That was Monday.

One of the things we had done in preparation for our walk was to talk to as many people as we could who had walked across America or at least done long-distance walking. It turned out that two of the people God allowed us to talk to had walked the entire length of Route 66. Their information was invaluable, and we actually used some of their notes and maps. One of the things both had told us was that when we got to the United States Marine Corps Logistics Base just outside of Barstow, California, we'd have to drive around it. Old 66 goes right through the middle of the base and no non-military personnel are allowed. Jane and I had committed to walk every step of the way, so we decided to go to the gate and ask if we could walk through. I took a brochure about the walk up to the Military Police officer on duty and explained what we were doing. He said he had no problem with it, but we'd have to check with the MP on duty the next day when we needed to walk through the base. Jane and I prayed about it because we felt two things very strongly. One, it was important to at least make an honest effort to walk every step. If we couldn't, we couldn't, but we needed to give it our best shot. Two, we wanted to walk through the base to pray for our men and women in the military. This became an important theme for us during the walk and one which afforded us many opportunities to share the gospel with active military personnel and veterans.

We walked up to the MP the next day and told him what we were doing, and he allowed us to go on in. The base was two miles long with no exit which meant we'd need to turn around and walk two miles out. Jane had developed blisters the second week, and her feet were hurting so badly she could hardly walk. She started praying as soon as we turned around that someone would give us a ride out, so we wouldn't have to walk the length of the base twice. A young woman named Lindsay was sitting at a stop sign inside the base, so Jane asked her if she'd give us a ride back to the gate. She said she'd be glad to. We got to talk to her about Jesus and she told us about her two sons, K.J. and Ronan. We told her we'd pray for her whole family.

After walking through the base, we stopped for lunch. Jane took off her shoes and socks to look at the blister on her foot. It was as big as a half dollar and full. I used a knife to relieve the pressure and empty it. We applied medicine and a bandage which didn't do much to alleviate the pain. The sunbaked Portland cement used to pave Route 66 was like a hot griddle and walking on it was torturous when it came to blistered feet. This was only one of the things we were never warned about and one, had we known about in advance, might have deterred us from starting the journey. People always say they'd like to be able to see the future, but honestly, had we seen all that was ahead of us on January 1st, we would likely never have taken the first step.

Later that afternoon we were walking out in the middle of the desert when a car pulled up beside us. Inside were a bubbly Hispanic woman and her Bichon Frise dog.

"Where are you going?"

"We're walking across America."

"I knew it. God told me to stop."

As it turned out this was a pretty good representation of how the next thirty minutes or so would go. She was full of excitement which came from being totally in love with Jesus. She talked 90 miles per hour with a thick accent and Jane and I were so "pumped" as Rose and Misty (the Bichon) drove off; we felt like we could walk another 20 miles despite Jane's pain.

What had just happened turned out to be a predictable pattern during the walk. There were times when we felt so tired and exhausted, we weren't sure we could walk another step. Then we'd have an encounter with someone like Rose. Sometimes it was a couple of minutes and other times twenty or thirty minutes, but invariably we would leave those encounters reenergized and ready to walk again.

We would hear from Rose several more times in the next few days. At one point she was ready to buy an old van, throw a mattress in the back and join us on the walk. Her husband discouraged it, I think. About a week later Rose called and said she was on the way to see us. It was about a one-hundred-mile drive. When she arrived, she had gifts for Jane and me and some homemade tamales. Rose would become a dear friend, calling every few weeks with prayer requests for her and her family and encouraging words for us.

Later that week, as we continued further into the desert, we came upon two dune buggies pulled off to the side of the road. As we walked past, we spoke to the three men and a woman standing beside the road. They were on their way to Laughlin, Nevada for a dune buggy race and one of their friends had had a flat tire in the desert. They were waiting for him to arrive so that they could continue. We saw this sort of thing over and over. They thought they were waiting for their friend, but really, they were waiting for us. They just didn't know it. It was what we would come to expect every day, divine appointments with people we didn't know but that God knew needed to hear about Him. We shared about our walk and about Jesus, gave them cards and walked on. Just as we were walking away, their friend arrived, and they took off through the desert. They honked and waved as they went by, leaving us in a cloud of dust.

Most of the people we talked to along the way we never heard from again. The folks in the dune buggies were no exception. We hoped we had planted some seed or watered some, but knew that whatever God had in mind for this encounter, we had been obedient by sharing the Truth with them in a casual way.

Imagine our surprise and delight when I opened my email on May 30th, nearly five months later and got this note.

Hello,

I was searching the internet for some recipes on cooking and was bored when I all of a sudden realized that on Jan. 14 I went on an off-road expedition from Landers, California to Laughlin, Nevada and that I had met a couple who were walking in the desert on route 66.

All I could think of is that these people are crazy and maybe even lost or broken down. When you two approached us we were shocked on the story that you guys told us about your mission. I thought in the back of my head that it was a crazy idea. You guys gave me your business card and during the remainder of our expedition that day to Laughlin I had lost it. Months went by and today I just for some reason decided to try and search for you guys and see how far you have gotten. As I searched on Google, I found a web site that rung a bell and I clicked on it, and sure enough it was the same couple I saw in the desert. I then proceeded to scan the web site and looked under updates and saw an article about Jan. 14 and read into it and noticed you had mentioned stumbling upon some off-roaders and I was completely shocked when I read it. I didn't even think you guys would remember us at all. I am writing this letter to inform you of our names and also to congratulate you on your accomplishments and God bless. Names are as follows: Jose, Tom, Kelly, and Greg.

All across the country, we left a trail of people like this; thousands of people. Some conversations started because of flat tires, or the weather, or a parent's experience raising their children. But regardless of how the conversations started, it always ended up being about Jesus. We didn't hear back from everyone we talked to, but we did hear from a lot of folks. Hopefully, others heard about us again on the news or read about us in a newspaper article. We prayed it would remind them of what we told them about Him. I think some people wondered why television coverage, radio interviews, and newspaper articles were so essential to our purpose. It was because each of those media exposures gave us one more platform to talk about Jesus. Most of us miss those opportunities several times a day. I'm sure we missed some too, but the desire of our hearts really was to make it all about Him.

It was a long week in the desert. By Friday afternoon we were glad to see a truck stop come into view, near the end of our day. Restrooms are few and far between in the desert and after a quick break, we felt refreshed enough to walk the last mile or so of the day. As we headed out of the parking lot, we heard someone yelling. We turned around and saw a man running toward us.

"It's you guys. It's really you."

We were puzzled.

"I was just crawling back into my sleeper to get some rest and I saw you walking. I wasn't sure it was you, so I grabbed the card you gave me and looked. Sure enough, it was you."

By this time, we had looked back across the parking lot and recognized the Werner truck. It was Mike "the U-turn truck driver". We were a hundred miles down the road and at just the right time, God had ordered our steps and Mike's big rig, to cross paths again. We were thrilled and shocked, but you should have seen Mike. He knew the chances were one in a million and he knew it was God.

"I've been thinking about what you said to me the other day. I've decided I need to get back with the Lord. I've thought a lot about you two."

We spent a few minutes with Mike before he went back and climbed into his cab to sleep. We encouraged him to begin sharing with other truckers about Jesus. He said he would. Somehow, I always thought we'd see Mike a third time, and we may have because after that day, truck drivers, especially Werner drivers, were always honking and waving. As a matter of fact, we were told several times during the walk that the truck drivers talked about us on the CB radios as we walked down the road. It was just one more way the word was getting out and people were finding out about what God had called us to do.

We had looked at the next section of old Route 66 on our maps for over a year. Several other walkers had told us this would be one of the most remote portions of the old route we would walk and, the most difficult part of the Mojave Desert to traverse. We would start on Saturday morning and then have a day to rest before conquering the remainder next week.

It's hard to understand how badly your feet can hurt when they are covered with blisters. My feet had healed well and were no longer a problem. I was now coating them in Vaseline several times a day to prevent my blisters from returning. However, the Vaseline didn't work for Jane and she was having a very hard time walking. Route 66 was deteriorating with practically every mile into a very rough, gravelly kind of surface. The rougher the surface the more painful it was for Jane to walk. She would sometimes be in such pain that I would cry as we walked because I knew the sacrifice she was making.

On Saturday morning we were driving out to the starting point to begin our journey toward Amboy, California. Jane is a very strong woman and has a very high tolerance for pain. She doesn't give up, not ever. But Jane was in such pain on Saturday morning from just putting her socks and shoes on that I was not sure she could walk. Honestly, she wasn't sure either.

On the way to walk, we listened to worship music, trying to ready our spirits for the day. I turned around to check on Jane because she wasn't singing, which was very unusual. She was quietly weeping, holding her hands up to the Lord. As she sat in His presence, I tell you, she glowed. When we arrived at our location we got out of the van and joined hands for prayer as always. When I was done praying, Jane said, "Honey, it's raining." She was feeling "raindrops" on her head, but it wasn't raining. She was in the presence of the Lord as I have rarely seen anyone. It was a special gift from God. It was what she needed for that day. She took off down the road by my side and we walked 12.3 miles.

This certainly would not be the last time we walked in God's presence. We found His presence repeatedly confirmed, and always, just when we needed assurance the most. Some people get a little skeptical when you talk about the presence of God. I think that's probably because most people don't make it a point to be aware of His nearness. It's not spooky or scary. It's actually calming and brings peace that nothing else can. After a while, we just made it a point to look for Him and to draw comfort and strength from His presence. It was a big part of the adventure. And…so we walked.

Chapter 6

The road to Amboy and beyond was every bit as remote as we had been told. When we got to Amboy it was truly a "ghost town". The restaurants, gas stations, and even a small elementary school were all closed. Tumbleweed danced across the parking lots of the buildings in town and plywood covered the doors and windows as if no one ever planned to return.

But even in Amboy, a car pulled into an abandoned gas station and we got an opportunity to share. As we were leaving town, a car pulled off to the side of the road to ask us for directions. Cairo, a young African American woman, was lost and almost out of gas. She needed to know the quickest way back to civilization. It was so weird because she had a notebook with the exact directions written down, yet she was bewildered, almost like she was blinded to what was written on the page. We knew God had arranged this divine appointment and soon knew why. Cairo said she was a Christian but quickly added she was not living for God and knew she needed to be. We encouraged her to renew her commitment to the Lord and told her we'd be praying for her, which we began doing as soon as she drove away.

Over the course of the walk, there were hundreds of examples of God bringing people to us. The ones in the middle of the Mojave Desert were some of the most obvious, but they happened repeatedly all across the country.

For example, as we walked between Amboy and Essex, California that week, we kept seeing semi-trucks carrying gravel.

There were always two of them. The first few times they passed us, they were pretty close and actually buzzed us. But as they kept passing us over the next three days, they gave us more and more room and then began to wave and smile. Finally, they even began to honk. On Wednesday morning, they passed us again, honked, waved, and smiled. As they roared by, Jane said, "I wish we could share with those drivers what we're doing and why." Then she quickly corrected herself and said she was not going to wish for it; she was going to pray for it.

Less than an hour later, just as we came into Essex, we heard this roar behind our heads and the loud hiss of air brakes. We turned around, and there were the two trucks that had been passing us all week, stopped right in the middle of Route 66. The drivers both jumped out of their trucks and started asking questions before their feet hit the ground.

"Where in the world are you guys walking? We've been seeing you for days."

"Washington D.C.!" we said.

Well, to make a long story short, we got the opportunity to share the gospel with one of the drivers who wasn't a Christian and encourage the one who, by his own admission, was a Christian but "not a very good one."

By this point in the walk, Jane had gotten unbelievably bold. She got in the Christian man's face and told him his friend needed to know Jesus and that it was his responsibility to live right in front of him, be a witness and share the gospel with him. Jane shook her finger in the faces of these two burly truck drivers standing in the middle of the road, shaking their heads in agreement. They hung their heads as if their mother was scolding them. I just stood there again with my mouth hanging open, thinking, "What could be better than this? This is really something." It still brings a smile to my face every time I remember it.

Considering that we saw people every single day on this deserted highway, which now serves only local traffic, it was miraculous. It was even more impressive that every person we met, with no exceptions, permitted us to talk with them about having a personal relationship with Christ. We knew God had asked us to do what we were doing. We knew that because of our willingness to obey, He was bringing people across our path so we could share the gospel. But I was about to discover something about the walk that would even shock me.

The story I'm getting ready to tell won't be for everyone. I've only told it to a very few people since it happened in January 2006. You'll probably want to skip to the next section if you have a problem with the supernatural or anything that can't be explained or proven scientifically. I even wrestled with whether to share it here. But it is part of the experience, and honestly, it was so personally important to me that it became one of the pivotal points of the walk. From that point on, I could look back and draw strength from it, and I believe it would leave the story partially untold if it were not shared.

As we continued walking through the desert, there were times when it would get utterly quiet. There was no traffic, no trains, no talking, just silence. It was during one of those times that it happened. There was no traffic, so we were walking on the road itself. Our steps made virtually no sound. We had learned from several days in the desert that when you did step off into the sand, your steps made a crunching sound. Well, Jane and I were walking. It was completely silent and then I heard footsteps. I honestly thought that somehow a hitchhiker or someone else had been able to sneak up beside us. I turned around so quickly that it hurt my neck. I was more than a little startled and maybe a little scared someone could get that close without us hearing them. When I turned around (I could still hear each step very distinctly crunching in the sand), no one was there. Believe it or not, I was quite relieved. I knew someone was walking beside us and the fact I couldn't see him just meant one thing to me. It had to be an angel. Every morning we prayed for angels to walk with us, protect and guide us. I'm not a big "angel nut." I mean, I'm not always seeing or talking about angels, but I do believe in their presence and am not surprised when they seem to be around. So, I told Jane, "An angel is walking with us."

"How do you know?" she asked.

"I can hear his footsteps."

"OK. Great," she answered nonchalantly.

That was it. He seemed to come and go several times during the day. I figured there was a good reason. Maybe there was some danger we weren't aware of, and he was there to protect us. Or perhaps he was there so we'd know he was there as we walked through the desert. I didn't make much of it until that evening at camp when I opened my email.

Rick/Jane,

We continue to pray for you each day. I can

just picture Jesus walking right alongside

you every step of the way.

Ron and Betty Teed

I said Ron was a friend, but truthfully, I'd never met him before. He found out about the walk through a radio news story and volunteered with his wife to come from the Chicago area and drive for us in Arizona and New Mexico. Both are highly educated, level-headed people, not given to hyperbole or even snake handling, as far as I know. They had no idea of our experience and since I have gotten to know Ron and Betty, I'd say they probably wrote what they felt they were supposed to write in the email. To be honest, I'm not sure who was walking alongside us that day. In the end, it may not matter. Either way, I am deeply honored that I was allowed to hear heavenly footsteps. I'm inclined to think it was Jesus. I know he's got a lot of other stuff going on in heaven and all, but I think sometimes he probably just drops in for a visit to let us know He's close by and cares. After all, it certainly wouldn't be the first time he'd walked through the desert.

This week would be one of the longest mileage weeks of the walk. Through trial-and-error experimentation, we got an efficient daily routine down. There were no populated areas to walk through during the entire week, so we spent most of our time walking. We would walk the farthest of any one day of the entire walk on Wednesday, 23.2 miles. But we would also decide to make an unexpected route change late in the week.

We continued to pour over maps and plan for the next day's walk during the evening hours. Old Route 66 had turned out to be a more significant challenge than we had ever dreamed. From the beginning of the walk, I had known that the approach to Needles might be a problem. The old route is gone, and the alternative was either Interstate or railroad tracks. I also knew the road from Needles up through Oatman, Arizona, and into Kingman looked very bad on our maps, and all our scouting reports were very pessimistic.

After another phone call and looking at the maps one last time, we decided to take the northern route into Kingman, which would accomplish two important things. One, we would miss the treacherous mountain pass through Oatman, and two; we would be able to walk through a few miles of Nevada. We felt any additional state where we could put the soles of our feet down was a plus.

When walking from West to East, one of the goals is to walk as few north-south miles as possible. Some are inevitable, like from Victorville to Barstow, California, but now we were deliberately choosing to walk some north-south miles. Quite frankly, I was a little tentative when we made the decision. As it turned out, it was precisely the right choice. Don't get me wrong, these were challenging miles, including two of the longest and steepest climbs of the entire walk. But for the most part, the roads were good, the shoulders were wide, and the Highway Patrol officers were some of the nicest in the country.

One exception to the wide shoulders was a short stretch of highway just after we turned north. Instead of a paved shoulder, it was soft sand and was almost like walking on a beach. As we were walking, I looked down and saw a golf ball. I stopped and picked it up. Written on the side of the brand-new golf ball in black magic marker was the name "Chuck." I stuck the ball in my pocket and continued to walk. Half a mile or so down the road, I spotted another golf ball. I picked it up, and it also said "Chuck." Jane and I were a little curious at this point and discussed what this was all about. We decided someone named "Chuck" must need prayer today, so we started praying for all the Chucks we knew. Over the next couple of miles, we found five identical golf balls, all with the name "Chuck" written on the side. We thought of our friend Chuck in Saratoga, Wyoming, so we started praying for him. Later in the week, I called Chuck to check on him and told him the story of the golf balls. Chuck said he had some medical issues and was going to the doctor for tests. He thanked us for our prayers.

The golf balls taught us a valuable lesson early in the walk. Whenever we saw a street name, a business name, a sign, or even a truck with something that reminded us of someone, we'd call out their name and pray for them on the spot. This happened hundreds of times during the walk. For example, whenever we see a Werner truck, we'd yell out, "Pray for Mike." Mike got prayed for hundreds of times that way. (As a matter of fact, many years later, we still pray for Mike every time we see a blue Werner truck). Two other times we had "Chuck" experiences. One time we were walking in a construction zone along an Interstate highway. We looked down in some bushes and saw a hard hat. On the front of the hard hat was written in black magic marker, in what looked like the same handwriting as the golf balls, "Chuck." This was several states and hundreds of miles away. Another day, we walked through a business district and saw one of those signs with changeable letters. All the letters had been scrambled, except in the middle of the sign where the name "Chuck" had been arranged. Needless to say, "Chuck" got lots of prayers on those days too.

We determined that the Lord uses lots of things to remind us to pray for people in need. We miss many things He puts in our path to bring people or situations to mind. I think we learned to be much more observant and hopefully more sensitive about God's promptings to pray for others. Many people told us after the walk that our names had also been brought to their minds and hearts. They didn't know why, but they prayed, and many of those prayers came at the most crucial times of the journey.

By the end of the week, we had crossed several milestones. We had finished our first state, California, and our second, Nevada, even though it was just a few miles. By lunchtime on Saturday, we crossed into Bullhead City, Arizona, our third state. We were now a little over ten percent of the way to Washington, DC.

Sunday morning, we attended a little Assembly of God church in Needles, California, where we had been camped for the week. We had contacted them the previous day about coming to their service and sharing about our journey. We walked in, dressed alike in America's colors and found about 20 people gathered there to worship. There were no musicians, and they sang to pre-recorded tapes. The pastor had graciously agreed to give us 10 minutes to share in the service. After the singing, the pastor introduced us and gave us the platform. When our ten minutes were up, he asked us to continue for the remainder of the service. At the end of our talk, he announced that the morning offering would come to us. This was totally unexpected, and we had not asked for anything except a few minutes to share. They took the offering and handed us an envelope full of cash at the end of the service. Jane tucked it away to open it later.

Meanwhile, the pastor encouraged the congregation to continue praying that they could purchase the property across the street, which was next to the local tavern. We suggested we prayer-walk the property with them and claim it for the Lord. We led them as they walked in circles around the corner lot, asking God to "deliver the land" into their hands to be used for the kingdom of God. What a glorious experience it was.

As we were driving to the campground for the following week, Jane pulled out the envelope and opened it. With about 20 people present, we didn't see how there could be much in the offering. To our amazement, one of the envelopes contained six one-hundred-dollar bills. Over seven hundred dollars total! God was only beginning to show his faithfulness in providing for our needs.

We reevaluated the call to walk across America many times throughout the first few weeks. Jane was in such pain nearly every day that it made me question the wisdom of her walking with me. We both felt the call and believed a spiritual principle was involved. The Bible talks about two people "touching" things together in prayer. We were convinced that we both needed to "touch" the ground together as we prayed for our country. I knew Jane would never ask to be released from her commitment, but I could not imagine how she could continue to walk. Nearly every day, there were new blisters. She was using boxes of Band-Aids® and bottles of powder, changing socks several times a day, soaking her feet in Epsom salt water every night, rubbing creams on her sore muscles and still, many nights she would lay down in bed and begin to cry because of the pain. I would get up, rub her legs, and then go to bed crying myself because I knew she was hurting. Several times during those early weeks, I told her she could stop and that I could walk alone, but she wouldn't hear of it. I must admit, several times; I tried to think of ways to stop the walk with grace so that I could stop her agony. Every time I came close to calling it quits, something would happen which would call me back to the reason we were walking in the first place.

I knew many people ahead needed to hear the good news of Jesus. I knew there were believers who needed to be encouraged in their lives. I knew there were many prayers that still needed to be prayed. God was showing us every day new ways to pray. We prayed for the children and the teachers when we passed a school. When we passed a church, we prayed for the pastor and congregation. When we walked past a white cross, we prayed for the family who had been left behind in grief. There was still much for us to do. We couldn't quit. And…so we walked.

Chapter 7

Of all the misconceptions about the walk we had beforehand, the worst may have been the idea that it was about the work *we* had to do. Please don't misunderstand. There was and still is much to do. The Lord of the harvest is always in need of laborers, those to do the work. But our shallowness and self-centeredness show through when we fail to realize first that it is His work, not ours we are called to do. The difference between those two perspectives is not insignificant. The plans He has for us are His plans. Our plans will most certainly fail, given enough time. It is when we step into His plans and take up the role He has chosen and enabled us to do, that His purpose will be accomplished.

Secondly, we had, and quite frankly, I think that most of us share this misconception, the notion that completing this task was about how our obedience would affect others. The truth is, obedience done with the servant's spirit will always affect us to a much greater degree than it affects others.

I think a perfect illustration of this is the example of washing feet. I was not raised in a denomination that practiced foot washing. I had never even seen it done. One Sunday morning during my quiet time, several years before the walk, I really sensed we should wash feet that Sunday morning in the church service. It was a radical thought for me, but I knew it was the Lord speaking. Our small church was meeting in homes for the summer because our building was not air-conditioned and unbearably hot. I called our house church host for the day and asked if he had an old washtub. He did, so at the end of our service I explained my understanding of the practice. I invited anyone who wanted to participate to ask the Lord whose feet they were to wash and invite them to the tub. I must tell you it was one of the most meaningful experiences of my Christian life. It was years before I did it again, but it was what God wanted for that day.

For me, at least, the experience of foot washing was not about the benefit the "washee" got from having their feet washed. It was about absolute obedience in the spirit of a servant, to give myself over to what God had called me to do…to wash someone else's feet.

Similarly, the walk across America, we discovered, was not always about how our obedience was affecting others, but how it was affecting us. We were being changed with every step we took. I began to see how painfully short I was falling every day of who God wanted me to be. I was less and less satisfied with my actions and attitudes.

One of the first areas I became aware of was with my role as a husband. Jane and I have a wonderful marriage. When we began the walk, we had been married for thirty-one and a half years. We get along remarkably well most of the time considering how much time we spend together. I noticed though, as we walked together, prayed together, discussed Scripture together, hurt together, and overcame obstacles together, I was becoming a more loving, caring husband. I became a more sensitive and loving man. When Jane was hurting, I helped with the laundry and the dishes. I ran the hot water for her feet and tried to help with the meals. I just wanted to do anything I could to help alleviate her pain. Nobody told me to. Jane didn't ask me to. I just wanted to. My desire to serve was being increased. My heart was more tender to the needs around me.

At the same time, I was seeing the areas where I was still failing as a husband. I was aware when my words were unkind, or sat like a lump while Jane was doing something for me I could have done for myself. I didn't and still don't do it all right, but I'm much more convicted than I have ever been.

Change, or transformation, when brought about through spiritual obedience, always leads to repentance. We understood our call to walk was a call to reclaim America. We learned very quickly that to reclaim what has been lost, you must deal with the sin which caused you to lose it in the first place. Dealing with sin means repentance. This necessary step is the step of repentance that keeps us from reclaiming our lives, our churches, our communities, and our nation for God. Perhaps the most dramatic example of this was what happened as we took the "big loop" of Old Route 66 from Kingman to Seligman, Arizona.

Jane and I had mixed emotions as we neared the Native American reservations of Arizona. We spent several weeks during the preceding five summers serving children in the Navajo Nation. We had learned just a little of the history of these wonderfully sweet people and the horrible mistreatment and injustice done to them. As we prepared to walk through their homelands, we both knew God would need to prepare our hearts for the mission. As we arrived at the sign welcoming us to the Hualapai reservation, we stopped. We bowed our heads, with tears in our eyes and cried out to God for forgiveness. Although we were not personally responsible for the Native American people's plight, we asked God to break our hearts for them and expose any unknown prejudice we may have harbored. We asked God to forgive our nation for all the injustices done to people of all colors and heal our land. I cannot explain to you in theological or even practical terms what happened during that prayer. I can only tell you a place in my heart became more tender toward others than it had ever been.

Just a few miles down the road we met Wallace, a Native American from the Havasupai tribe. Wallace was yet another example of someone just standing by the side of the road, seemingly waiting for us to show up. I immediately sensed my heart was different. I wanted to talk with Wallace, and I was genuinely interested in his life. He told us a horrific story we would hear repeated many times throughout the walk. Wallace, who was 54 years old, had been taken from his family at age six and relocated to another state to a "religious" center to be educated. He was taught religious doctrine, baptized into a "church", and educated in the ways of his "captors" (my word). His mouth was washed out with soap whenever he spoke his native language to encourage him to speak English. He was beaten and abused when he did what was not acceptable. Amazingly, this was all done in the name of God. Eventually, Wallace and the other children were returned to their homes and families, albeit scarred for life by their treatment.

Wallace served his country in the military during the last years of the Vietnam War. He had worked as a productive citizen and loved his country, despite its treatment of his people. He is the kind of person we'd all like to have as a friend or a neighbor. When it came to sharing our faith with Wallace, we had a huge obstacle. The obstacle was history. Our nation's history, his own personal history, and the "church's" history had all left Wallace wounded. Right then and there, Jane and I took our prayer a step further. We told him how sorry we were for the way he was treated and for how his people had been so wronged. Wallace's wall of resistance to the gospel melted away, almost instantly. We had no ulterior motives. We did what we did because our hearts were moved with compassion for a people wronged. I think Wallace saw that in our eyes and then allowed us to share the love of God with him. We stood in the middle of the Arizona desert and shared with Wallace for about 30 minutes, an unheard-of length of time when you're trying to cover 20 miles per day on foot. Before we left, he asked us if we could send him a Bible. He and his people live at the bottom of the Grand Canyon and mail is delivered either by mule or helicopter. We sent Wallace a Bible and rejoiced when we received a thank you note several months later, sent from the bottom of the Canyon signed by Wallace Senyela.

As we walked away from Wallace, it began to snow. The pure white flakes reinforced our feeling that something cathartic and cleansing had happened. We would never again look at anyone in the same way. We were beginning to see people through the eyes of Jesus. The walk was changing us from the inside out and in ways that could only be accomplished one day at a time…one step at a time. And…so we walked.

Chapter 8

It never ceased to amaze us how desperately God desired to speak to some people. It was apparent He had gone to great lengths to cause our path to cross theirs. In some instances, we were just one link in a chain of people God had arranged to speak to them. Such was the case with Karen Landis. As we approached Seligman, Arizona, our driver had pulled into a wide driveway for our lunch break. Just about the time we got settled in for lunch, the person who lived at the ranch house came home. Karen got out of her truck and we called out to her to tell her what we were doing and make sure it was okay to eat lunch there. She said yes. A little later she came out to chat a bit and we were able to share with her about the walk across America. Karen told us that a few years earlier a Christian man riding his bike across America to share his faith had also stopped at her house for lunch. We thought it was amazing God had arranged for two cross-country travelers to stop at this particular ranch house to eat lunch and of course, to share His love with this woman.

We were reminded again and again of God's hand in the walk as we saw these encounters unfold. Things you would never expect to happen…happened. Just after we left Karen Landis' house, a huge tour bus came to a stop in the middle of Route 66 to make sure we were okay. As Jane yelled up to the driver and gave him a card, the whole bus erupted in cheers and applause. We shared with two highway department workers, Deborah and Andrea, who were picking up trash in a rest area. They drove up just as we were arriving and drove away just after we left. God's timing was always perfect. As we approached

Parks, Arizona, a woman we called Blessing was out at the end of her driveway talking on her cell phone. She was not a believer but listened politely as we talked about Jesus. God doubled our witness at this stop since Blessing's friend China could hear everything we shared through the cell phone.

As we walked through the tall pines, just outside the picturesque, shop-filled village of Williams, Arizona, Sarah, a local police officer, pulled up beside us and rolled down her window. When we shared with her why we were walking, her huge smile made us wonder if she was a fellow believer. When we asked her about Jesus, she assured us of her relationship with Him, which gave us great encouragement for the day.

The more we walked, the more opportunities we saw to share God's love. When asking directions from someone, we always tried to reflect the Lord's love and respect for people. We did not seek out people with physical or mental disabilities, but we often talked with them about the walk. We tried particularly hard to be respectful and tender with those who had special challenges. No one was exempt from our sharing. Cashiers, gas station attendants, children, construction workers, and waitresses were all crossing our path for a reason. One day near Winona, Arizona we saw some electric company workers in a cherry picker working on the lines. Jane yelled up and began chatting with them about Jesus. Back and forth the conversation went up and down from 20 or 25 feet off the ground. The opportunities were almost endless. As a matter of fact, there were days when we were more exhausted from sharing than from walking.

This happened most often in and around larger cities with higher concentrations of people. Sometimes we would literally go from one person to the next with just a few steps in between. Such was the case in Flagstaff, Arizona. As we walked through the city it was warm, sunny and dry. It was perfect weather for the homeless. It had been an exceptionally mild winter in Arizona and many of the homeless who usually would have gone even further south were still here in early February. An interesting side note was that we had been praying for nearly a year that the weather would be mild enough to make the walk possible for two amateurs. Snow in the mountains would have made it extremely difficult to climb the steep grades. The downside to our answered prayers was that many of the ski resorts had been unable to open or had had to close early. We earnestly apologized to those who rely on the tourist trade from skiers as we walked through little towns like Williams, Arizona. We also promised that as soon as we were out of town, we'd pray for snow. We honored that promise and heard that behind us it had started to snow in the mountains and ski resorts were reopening!

I was nearing the end of a very difficult week. We had walked at 7000 feet and above, crossed the 500-mile mark, endured some very rugged roads through the mountains, walked several miles on railroad tracks, spent many hours scouting out paths, had some encounters with wild pigs and dogs and Jane had suffered with blisters all week.

As we began walking Friday morning, we started running into people one right after another. There were people on their way to work, a Native American family who needed furniture and a car, a young Hispanic man who looked like a gang member, an emotionally unstable man, and then there was Will and Linnea.

Will and Linnea, a young couple in their early twenties, crossed the street right in front of us and walked toward us. Both had multiple piercings in their eyebrows, lips, noses, ears, and tongues. Linnea had a black eye and deep scratches on her face. Their clothes were dirty, and they carried well-worn backpacks, an almost certain giveaway of their homelessness. As we met on the sidewalk, all four of us stopped and began a conversation. After a few minutes, we found out they were indeed living on the streets and trying to get enough money for a room for the night. We gave them a few dollars and asked them if we could pray with them. On Route 66 in the middle of Flagstaff, we put our arms around Will and Linnea and prayed with them. We lifted our heads and prepared to say goodbye. We noticed they were both visibly moved and Linnea had tears rolling down through the scratches on her cheeks.

We gave them both a hug and turned to walk on. Jane mentioned we should have bought them a meal, so I suggested we pray God would let us see them a second time (almost unheard of when you're walking across America), so we could bless them again.

The next day, Saturday morning, we were out looking for a place to attend church on Sunday. As we were driving down the street, we saw Will and Linnea rounding a corner. They saw us at about the same time and we quickly turned into a parking lot. They ran to see us, and both gave us and our driver (whom they had never met) hugs. They were excited to tell us they'd been able to get a place to sleep the night before and had also found temporary jobs washing dishes at the local university. We shared for a few minutes and gave them our cell phone number. We told them we'd be camping in Flagstaff for a few days and if they needed anything to let us know.

That afternoon the phone rang. Will wanted to know if we could pick them up at work late that night and give them a ride back across town to their motel. Of course, we agreed, even though it was going to be way past our bedtime. We figured God had given us a third opportunity to sow into Will and Linnea's lives and we didn't want to miss out on it.

We picked up our new friends from work and took them to Jack In The Box for burgers. While driving back to their motel, Will told us he had called his mother to tell her about meeting us. She was evidently a godly woman who'd been praying for her son. He told us his mom said we were an answer to her prayers. Will said, "My mom said she's been praying that God would send someone to cross my path to remind me Jesus loves me. She says you're the ones He sent."

When we pulled up to the motel, we could hardly believe the horribly run-down place where they were staying. I had to fight back the tears as we left them. We invited them to church the next morning and said goodbye once again.

Sunday morning when we pulled into the church parking lot Will and Linnea were sitting on the curb. Never before or never again would we see someone on four different occasions during the walk. Will and Linnea slipped out before the end of the service. When we got to the car there was a note printed on a napkin that read:

Thank you for your kindness and your prayers.

You will be in our hearts and prayers forever.

God bless you…and keep you

And cause His face to shine upon you.

Will and Linnea

Will and Linnea will always be in our hearts too.

We found most days would be about people like Will and Linnea and not about the miles. There were days when getting in the 20 miles was the primary focus. But most days were about the individuals who connected the miles together. Most were receptive to the message we shared. Most were interested in our story. Most were respectful of our faith and mission even if they were not believers. However, one of the saddest commentaries on the entire walk was that the least interested and least considerate were often those who should have cared the most. With only a few exceptions, the least receptive people were pastors and churches. We had been warned by a friend who had made a cross-country walk of his own that churches might not be very helpful on our journey. Our experience with churches was more positive than his and some congregations did help us with finances, drivers, and other means of support. But generally speaking, the people who should have been in harmony with our walk, or at least cared about their brother and sister in Christ, were sometimes…well, almost rude. I should point out we never asked for money or material help from pastors or churches. What we wanted from them more than anything else was just a little time to share about our walk and ask them to pray for us as we continued our journey. Many churches we called responded with something like, "We don't want anything to do with that."

The other purpose for connecting with churches was to see if there was anything we could do for them. When we approached a church building during the walk, we tried to meet the pastor. In keeping with one of the stated purposes for our walk, to encourage Christians, we would ask if there were any needs in the church about which we could join with them in prayer. Just outside of Flagstaff, Arizona we got one of the most unbelievable responses ever. After explaining who we were and what we were doing, we asked the pastor if he or the church needed prayer. His response was an emphatic "No"!

Jane and I left that building hurt and wounded, but more than anything else bewildered. What has hardened the hearts of so many believers? What would cause a spiritual leader of a congregation to be so offended by an offer of prayer? How has the family of God become so suspicious of anyone who does something out of the ordinary? These really weren't isolated incidents. Throughout the walk, we found a great amount of apathy and skepticism present in the Church. There were exceptions and there were local congregations that were open and supportive. The ministers who had led their congregations to have the heart of Jesus were easily recognized. The believers along the way who were striving to live out their faith in an authentic way were obvious. The opposite was equally evident.

It certainly gave us pause to consider how we were received by the poor, the homeless, and society's outcasts more readily than we were by our own spiritual family. Perhaps this was one of the reasons Jesus spent so much more time with sinners than the religious leaders of His day. Standing still to ponder this hard-heartedness provided no easy answers and so we continued. The answers always seemed to come through walking. And...so we walked.

Chapter 9

The range of emotions we felt on the walk across America was wide and deep. Sometimes we experienced sadness and grief because of the treatment and plight of many Americans. There were also times of joy and accomplishment as we were able to help someone buy a meal or bring a little happiness into their daily routine. Our idealism and patriotism certainly faded from time to time and our rock-solid convictions felt more like Jell-O some days. The pendulum would sometimes swing wide and fast as we moved between victory and defeat several times a day. There is no accurate way to describe with words what was happening at this point in the walk. Everything, every emotion, every pain, every frustration and every breakthrough was magnified. The variety, intensity, and enormity of the journey were starting to sink in. We were beginning our sixth week. The journey thus far had been more physically demanding than we could have possibly imagined. The phone calls of support from home had started to taper off. I was wondering if Jane's feet were ever going to heal. Week six gave us all these plus two new huge obstacles…no roads and no drivers.

Just outside of Winona, Arizona, old Route 66 becomes unpredictable. There were isolated pieces of it, but it was certainly not consistent. Many parts of the old road had been covered over when Interstate 40 was built. Some segments headed out into the desert, crumbled into gravel, disintegrated into sand and dirt, then ended at a barbed-wire fence. We walked on every kind of surface which would be represented in the entire walk this week, including many miles on

Interstate 40. This was some of the most frightening walking we did during the six months. For example, the Interstate bridged many canyons with only scant inches of shoulder. We had to run from one side of each bridge to the other to beat the semi-trucks which were approaching.

We also walked out through the desert following the remnants of the old 66. We logged many miles during week six on nothing but sand, one of the most tiring surfaces to traverse. We climbed over and under more barbed-wire fences during this week than any other. In addition, we walked railroad tracks and railroad service roads for miles. During these off-road treks of six to nine miles, it was not uncommon to see coyote and mountain lion paw prints in the dried mud. While walking on railroad tracks, we occasionally had to run across the trellises which spanned the canyons to keep from finding ourselves trapped in the middle, with a train coming.

The easiest walking was where the old road was still intact. This occurred most often around tourist attractions still holding on by a thread or in populated areas. But even then, there were challenges when we missed the road signs or got separated from drivers, which happened quite often in the cities.

During the walk's planning stages, we had gone through several versions of how the logistics of walking across America would work. We decided to camp approximately in the middle of where we would be walking each week and have our volunteer drivers shuttle us out in the morning, stay close with supplies, food, water, and rain gear during the day, and then shuttle us back to camp in the evening. In addition, drivers would need to scout out where we would be walking next, help calculate mileage walked each day, run errands while we walked, share the gospel with people they encountered along the way and explain to others what we were doing.

Walking without a driver left us at a huge disadvantage because it drastically reduced the number of miles we could walk in a day and left us without any supplies on hand, should we have an emergency. We had never been able to recruit volunteer drivers for week six. We were relying on one-day-at-a-time drivers which were secured through a local church in Flagstaff. We also had discovered that our ministry friends Randy and Marli Brown happened to be in the area, so Randy volunteered for one day as well. Every day of the week was spoken for except for Tuesday. It was very tempting to take the day off after an extremely tough day on Monday. We had walked the entire 21 miles on the Interstate and knew we had a lot of Interstate miles coming up later that week.

But Tuesday morning we got up at the usual time, 4 a.m., and got ready to walk. We kept thinking the phone would ring and someone would volunteer to drive. When it was time to go and no one had called, we decided to drive out to Winslow, Arizona. We would walk the miles which should be walked on Wednesday, thus reducing our chances of being stranded in the middle of the desert.

We had been praying for over a year God would direct our steps to intersect other's paths at just the right time to show and share with them the love of God. We took every variation from our predetermined plan very seriously. Delays or shuffling the schedule would not only affect the encounters that day but also the remainder of the trip. We tried not to be too fatalistic or let the schedule control us because we understood God was in control and could continue to alter not only our paths but the paths of others to accomplish His purpose. It boiled down to being sensitive to what God led us to do each day. There were days we felt we needed to stop short of our planned miles and days we felt we should walk further. It was amazing how many times we could see God's hand in it that day or the next or the next. Tuesday in Winslow, Arizona was definitely one of those days.

We drove out to Winslow and parked our van at a truck stop. We started walking west through town and saw a young Native American man with a backpack walking toward us on the other side of the street. His head was down. We called out to him and he acknowledged us with a half-hearted wave barely taking the time or effort to lift his head. As we continued to walk through Winslow, there were God-placed people everywhere. A young couple was getting into their car just as we walked past. A truck driver with a tire problem had pulled off into a parking lot right along our path. There was a crisis pregnancy center with an open sign, so we went in to introduce ourselves and share about our walk. In front of a flower shop there was a teenage boy. "I'm LDS," was his response to our question about whether he knew Jesus. (LDS is how many Mormons refer to themselves in the West.) Over and over again there were people in our path. Most of them were eager to talk and share, but none quite as talkative as Raymond and Celeste.

These two Native Americans, Raymond a Navajo and Celeste a Seneca, were sitting out in front of a senior citizens center in downtown Winslow. We stopped for a quick greeting but got much more than that. Raymond had a story to tell much like Wallace, the Havasupai, back near Seligman. He had also been taken away from his family, mistreated and abused by white people, all in the name of religion. Raymond had rejected Christianity (can you blame him?) and had determined to follow the Navajo religion. Once again, Jane and I were able to share with Raymond about how God had broken our hearts over what had been done in years past to the Native American people. You could tell from the expression on this old man's face he had never heard anything like this before. We shared with him that not everything Christian people do represents Jesus well. I talked with Raymond for a long time about how much God loves him, while Jane talked to Celeste. We both left saddened we couldn't undo in a few minutes what had been done over a lifetime to damage the perception of Christ in people like Raymond. All we could do is love and accept them and hope they saw a reflection of Jesus in us.

We had walked less than ten miles total, yet the day had slipped away. By taking so much time with each of our encounters, the miles had accumulated slowly. We started back toward the truck stop where we had parked the van. Just across the street from the truck stop was a "Welcome to Winslow" sign and some sort of memorial with a United States flag. As we walked past it, we noticed a man standing by the flagpole with his back to us. We couldn't resist the opportunity for one last encounter for the day and so we called up to the man. As he turned around, we realized this was the first young man we had seen as we entered town, the one who had barely acknowledged our greeting. We also noticed he was crying.

We began asking questions right away to see if there was anything we could do.

"Why are you crying? Is everything alright?" we asked.

"I was just remembering," the young man replied.

Rick, a Navajo, was standing between two beams from the World Trade Centers. He had been part of the Navajo Job Corps sent to New York City to help clean up the site of the terrorist attacks. Rick's job had been to sift through the debris looking for the dead.

"I was just remembering what it was like to find someone," Rick confessed with tears streaming down his cheeks.

Rick shared about his life after his job in New York City was over. He was now homeless, living out of a backpack under Interstate bridges. Our hearts broke again for a fellow American who had been treated so horribly and discarded so frequently by our society. (Except when we needed him to do something like sift through the rubble for dead bodies.) I thought each time I heard a story like Rick's I would be stronger. Maybe the next time I wouldn't be moved to tears and my heart wouldn't feel as though it was being ripped in two, but it never happened. Thank God, it never happened.

We asked Rick if there was anything we could do for him. He said he was awfully hungry. Hunger was one thing I knew how to fix. I knew the truck stop just across the street had a great buffet, so I offered to take Rick across the street for lunch.

As we started across the street, Rick said, "They won't let me eat in there."

"Why not?" I asked.

"Because I'm homeless and because I'm...an Indian." Rick's head was down again now.

I've lived a life virtually void of prejudice, which is why I was totally unprepared for what was about to happen.

"Well, let's just go see," I said as I tried to remain optimistic.

We walked into the truck stop and up to the cashier. I told her I wanted to buy my friend Rick the buffet for lunch. While I reached for my wallet, she reached for one of those white Styrofoam "to go" boxes. She said she was sure Rick would want his lunch to go.

I'd never been sure what righteous indignation meant until that moment. I felt a lot more love and compassion for Rick right then than I did for the cashier. I tried to remain calm and not let my new friend see my anger. I informed the cashier he'd be eating in, just like everyone else. I stayed until Rick was seated with his lunch and waved goodbye.

When I left, I prayed for Rick and others like him in this country who have been treated less than human just because of the color of their skin, a disability, or their nationality. I felt sorry for him. but I felt even worse for people like the cashier who reach for the "to go" boxes of life and never realize what they're doing.

There would be more ahead like Rick who were waiting to eat, waiting to be treated with dignity and love. Our nation was scattered with people, red, yellow, black and even white, who find themselves discarded by society. Some live under bridges, some in rat-infested slums, and some even blend in the best they can in our own neighborhoods. We had begun praying early in the walk God would give us the heart of Jesus, and it was happening. Every day, with every step, people were capturing our hearts.

Many times, when we told the story of Rick and others like him, people told us there weren't any folks like that in their city or town. The next day we would see them in an alley or behind a dumpster getting ready to find their next meal. Sometimes we saw the tell-tale signs of the homeless living under an overpass, sometimes within a few hundred feet of a church building. The truth was, they were there. It reminded me of how Jesus saw the blind and lame who His disciples had walked by for years, and never seen. So, now we asked God to give us the eyes of Jesus too, to help us see them; to find them along the way. And…so we walked.

Chapter 10

The sixth week had proven to be a challenge in many ways. One of the real challenges came on Friday. All week we spent a significant part of each day trying to find places to walk. Some days our drivers ventured out into the desert to scout our walking path only to have to turn around when the dirt path dead ended. The advice of locals when it came to roads was surprisingly unreliable. We tried to always confirm with at least two people that the road eventually led to our destination for the day. Despite our collection of maps and computer programs that we used in the evening to make plans for the next day, physically driving the route was the only reliable confirmation the road or path was still there.

On Friday morning we were beginning at the east edge of Joseph City, AZ. The problem was we just simply could not find a road to walk on. The locals had advised that we not walk on the Interstate for this stretch of ten miles or so to Holbrook. Although we had been given permission by the Arizona Department of Transportation to walk on I-40 when necessary, this was an especially treacherous section of the highway where trucks were coming downhill and around lots of hidden curves. Walking on the Interstate just didn't seem wise. We had searched the maps and driven around looking the night before, and yet arrived at the starting point Friday morning with no idea where to walk.

Our ending point on Thursday night was a truck stop and so we pulled into the same parking lot on Friday morning. I immediately started asking folks who lived in the area how we could get to Holbrook. Usually, someone knew of a back road or a farm road, but not today. What we heard over and over was what we already knew: the only road that went east toward Holbrook except the Interstate was the road that dead-ended into the Cholla Power Plant. That dead-end was accentuated with a wide metal gate that was chained and padlocked. The gate was also adorned with a large stop sign and a NO TRESPASSING sign.

We had determined early on that we would strive to obey the rules and follow the laws wherever we were. It was not always easy and some of the rules cost us a lot of miles, but we felt part of our witness was to be law-abiding. There were times when Route 66 ran into I-40 and the separation was a barbed-wire fence. We had permission to walk on both and climbing over or under the fence wasn't trespassing, it was just the quickest way between the two. We didn't have a problem with that sort of thing, but this was a huge gate and an emphatic sign which left no doubt about the legality of hopping the fence.

After spending what seemed like an unreasonable amount of time trying to find an alternative, we determined the Interstate was our only legal option. We went into the truck stop for a final restroom break before heading out for the morning. When I came out and headed toward the van, I heard someone call out to me. It was a woman sitting in her car. After filling her car with gas, she and her dog were ready to pull out. But, after overhearing my conversations, wanted to offer a solution.

"You can cross through the power plant," she said.

I explained to her what we were doing and why and then shared with her that we didn't want to trespass or do anything that would cast a bad reflection on the walk. She seemed to appreciate that and so she offered to get us permission to walk through the power plant property. She picked up her cell phone and called her husband, who just happened to be one of the plant managers. She told him what we were doing and asked him if he could get us clearance to walk through. Of course, I couldn't hear his end of the conversation, but I did hear hers.

"No honey, they're not drug dealers. They're nice people just like us," she explained while rolling her eyes.

Mrs. Hunt said they'd have the gate open by the time we got there. Then she told us her personal property backed up to the power plant and we could walk across her property up to the next exit, which by the way was called the Hunt Road exit.

We arrived at the gate, which was now open, and made our way through the opening into the power plant. What became apparent was that this road had been Route 66 many years before. When crews had built I-40, they had gone right over the top of the old 66. The power plant property was just a few feet from the Interstate highway. This was not the first or last time we would see this phenomenon. Especially in places where road building was a real challenge, like through a mountain pass. The old road served as a good foundation for one side of the new Interstate. It made perfect sense from an engineering point of view, but it presented a special challenge for cross-country walkers, from time to time.

We began winding our way through the power plant on the gravel road which led first beside the tall smokestacks and then several steaming lakes. It wasn't long before a white security truck pulled up beside us. Apparently, someone had opened the gate for us but had forgotten to tell the security guard about the special permission Mrs. Hunt had arranged for us.

"Out for a little exercise?" was the way Dave the security guard greeted us. He was trying to be friendly, but you could tell he wasn't very happy we were there.

"More than a little. We're walking across America," was my nervous response.

Dave was taken aback and temporarily forgot that as far as he knew we were trespassers. He wanted to know the details and started through the list of questions we had answered hundreds of times: When did you start? Where did you start? How long will it take you? Why are you doing it?

That's the question we always wanted to hear. When someone asked "why" you had an open door to tell them.

"We're walking across America to tell people about Jesus. Do you know Him?" was our provocative response.

Our conversation then turned toward things spiritual, and Dave affirmed he was a follower of Christ. He expressed a real interest in our walk and its purpose and wanted to have prayer before we walked on. Dave climbed out of the truck and we joined hands there on that chilly desert morning beside the steaming water. I prayed for Dave and for us and as happened so many times, our time of prayer together ended with hugs all around.

Dave wanted to know what we would do when we got to the edge of the power plant property. We told him Mrs. Hunt had called her husband and not only gotten us permission to walk through the power plant, but she had also given us her blessing to walk across their ranch, which was the next parcel of ground. At the mention of Mrs. Hunt's name, Dave seemed to sigh in relief as he suddenly remembered we were on private property. Dave assured us if the Hunts had given their permission, then all was well. He thought for a moment and realized crossing the Hunt ranch still wouldn't get us to Holbrook. Dave promised to take his upcoming coffee break and scout out a way to Holbrook. He promised to meet us on the other side of the Hunt estate.

Getting across the power plant's property lines and then across the ranch necessitated climbing several fences and gates. When we climbed the last one and started up the access road, Dave was sitting there in his pick-up truck. Dave had spent some time looking for the next piece of the puzzle to Holbrook and had found a way. At this point, we were less than half a mile from the railroad tracks which would lead us the last six miles right into Holbrook. At the tracks we said our final goodbyes to Dave, but not before one last prayer. This time Dave wanted to pray. There, among the desert flowers and discarded railroad ties, he prayed a blessing on us and thanked God for the opportunity to meet us. His prayer brought tears to my eyes as I thought of all the minute details that had fallen into place that week, making it possible for us to meet Dave.

The one-day-at-a-time drivers had altered our schedule. The driverless day in Winslow had delayed us by fifteen miles forward progress. Thursday was an excruciating day for Jane. She had walked a significant part of the morning in tears. Then that very morning at the truck stop, we spent half an hour trying to find an alternate route. Mrs. Hunt just "happened" to be in the right place at the right time to overhear my conversation. Dozens of things had happened that week to guide our steps and alter the timetable that had landed us exactly where Dave was at exactly the right moment. I was in awe of God's ordering of our steps once again. I knew the encounter with Dave was not an accident. I knew we were there for his benefit, and he had been there to encourage us. I knew we were serving a God who was intimately concerned with both our needs. I also knew we were serving a God who was so awesome He could work out all the details for it to happen. What an unbelievable day.

However, we didn't know until later just how special this encounter really had been and how necessary it was for us to meet Dave. A few days later when I checked my email, there was a note from our new friend at the Cholla Power Plant.

In the short email, Dave thanked us for spending time with him. He shared about the spiritual struggles he had been going through and why. In addition to losing his wife in a divorce, Dave had lost his only daughter in an automobile accident a couple of years before. The same year he had lost a sister-in-law, also in a car accident, his father died, and then his brother had been put in prison. Who could blame Dave for wondering where God was in all of that?

That morning, as Dave was driving around the power plant on his rounds, he wasn't just looking for trespassers. He was looking for answers. He was looking for confirmation God was still there and still cared. He was looking for a sign which would permit him to keep believing in the middle of all the junk life had thrown his way. And he found it. He found it when he pulled up beside two people walking through a power plant who had smiles on their faces and a message straight from heaven.

Others were hurting too. Others were searching for a sign. Others were looking for the answer we'd been privileged to carry across the nation. We knew God would orchestrate their steps to meet two travelers walking down the road. They didn't know it, but they were on a collision course for a God-sized encounter with the awesome message of His love. And…so we walked.

Chapter 11

Leaving Dave behind, we walked along the railroad tracks for about six more miles into Holbrook, Arizona. Along the way, as had happened before, we met men working on the railroad tracks. The Santa Fe Rail system employs people all along the route to maintain the tracks. In this part of the country, many of the workers are Hispanic and sometimes we weren't even sure they understood us when we explained what we were doing. We always wanted them to know we weren't going to try to hop on a train or interfere with their work in any way. On this occasion, when we told the workers what we were doing and why, they all wanted one of our business cards which had a picture of us walking. A few minutes after we left them, they returned and gave us some bottles of water with the railroad logo on the label. It was just one more example of how saying a kind word and treating people with respect, can mean so much to them and make a positive impression for the cause of Christ.

By this point in the walk, we realized how many people we pass by every day without giving it a thought. As we walked through the heart of Holbrook past the Wigwam Motel, we spoke with Leslie, an older woman crossing the street. Then we saw a lady fall in a car wash and went to see if she was hurt. We stopped by First Baptist Church and spoke with the janitor and then on to the eastern edge of town for lunch. There we were approached by Peterson Begay, a Navajo who had obviously been drinking. He was from Indian Wells, Arizona which is on the reservation. He asked for money, but instead, we called our drivers, offered him a ride to McDonald's and bought his lunch.

We gave him a couple of bottles of water and talked with him about Jesus. He invited us to his house, but we declined because it was a long drive into the reservation.

One of the few regrets we had all along the walk was we always seemed to be pressed for time. Our route had been laid out on a timeline we believed was inspired. We felt we needed to keep as close to the schedule as possible and as it turned out, we were right. Later in the walk, we would be so thankful we had walked long, hard days to stay on track. But on days like this, it was tempting to take a side trip into the reservation to visit Peterson's home and family. We would love to have gone to all the places we were invited. One of the dreams I have for the future is to take a year-long sabbatical to travel without a schedule and go wherever God opens a door. We'll see.

This week, with its one-day-at-a-time drivers, was almost over. On Saturday, we had a long drive from Flagstaff where we stayed longer than usual to connect with local church volunteers. It was ninety-five miles one way to the starting point for the day. Bob and Candy, our drivers for the day, followed us so we wouldn't have to drive back to Flagstaff after we finished walking. This saved us several hours of driving and indicated the kind of folks God brought into our lives to bless us and to make the walk possible. These folks not only did a lot of extra driving to help us, but did it sacrificially, on the first day of their vacation. In addition, they filled up our vehicles with gas, no small contribution.

With all the amazing experiences we were having as we walked, it was sometimes easy to become a bit disconnected from our "other life". It wasn't that we didn't think about home and family, because we did. But sometimes it was like we were living in another dimension. From time to time the cell phone would ring and on the other end would be the voice of someone jolting us back to reality. That was the case on this day.

We were literally walking through the middle of the desert. Route 66 had disappeared once again, so we ventured out on a sandy, telephone company access road. As we walked, we got further and further from the Interstate. First, we lost sight of it and then we couldn't even hear the traffic. It became apparent we had inadvertently wandered onto someone's ranch, so we started trying to get back to the highway. During this side trip our phone rang. It was our daughter, Rebekah. She was crying a little as she told us she was in bed suffering from a migraine. It's hard to explain, but you forget the walk at that moment, and you forget where you are. All you can think about is that your child is hurting. We stopped walking behind an old, abandoned barn and prayed with her on the phone. As soon as we hung up, I called my parents and asked them to pray. We started walking again, but now we were concentrating on more than getting back to the highway. We prayed as we walked, something which had become second nature to us. Finally, we could hear and then see the traffic on the Interstate. We made our way down to the barbed wire fence that separated the desert from the highway, scooted underneath and back onto the shoulder of the Intestate. Just as we did, the phone rang again. It was Rebekah. The headache had left as quickly as it had come.

I am not sure if it was because we were so "connected" to God during those months of walking that made our prayers more powerful, or that our hearts had become so tender we saw the hand of God more clearly. Whatever it was, Jane and I both acknowledge we have never been as close to God as we were during the walk across America. There was something about trusting Him for literally every step and every ounce of strength that drew us close to Him. This answer to prayer was just one of many examples in which God showed Himself faithful and powerful. Thankful for Rebekah's healing, we refocused and walked on toward the edge of the Petrified Forest, where we would end our walk for the week.

It was so great to begin the new week with drivers who we knew would be with us for an entire week. Most weeks it took a day or two for the drivers to get the hang of it and begin to feel comfortable with the responsibilities. When the drivers were only with us for a day or two, it seemed like we were spending a lot of time and energy training them. Ron and Betty Teed had driven from Wheaton, Illinois to help us out for a week. We had never met them before they arrived in Gallup, New Mexico, our camping base for the week. They heard about the walk on Moody Radio® and called to volunteer. It still amazes us that people we didn't even know came from all over the country to participate in the walk by driving our support vehicle.

All our drivers were a great help and most caught on quickly, but Ron and Betty made themselves at home and really became a part of our lives immediately. Looking back at it, it was a blessing they did because we were beginning what would be one of the busiest weeks of the walk.

This week we walked either on the Navajo reservation or very close to it. Not surprisingly, most of our encounters were with Navajos, beginning with the very first minutes on Monday morning. After a long drive to our starting point, we stopped at a Navajo trading post to use the restroom. Jane immediately struck up a conversation with one of the owners about Jesus. She had been told by her Native American church leaders that they taught the same things as the Bible. Yet, when Jane asked her if they taught about Jesus, God's Son who had come to earth to die on the cross, she said no. I was so proud of Jane as she lovingly talked with this Navajo woman about our Lord. Without judgment or criticism of her church, Jane shared the wonderfully good news of Jesus with her before we left.

As we walked on through the Petrified Forest on the Interstate, then on railroad tracks and dirt roads through the reservation, we noticed more and more Navajos were waving and smiling at us as they passed in their cars. This enthusiasm for our presence seemed more than a little odd to us. Two white people walking through the reservation would not normally expect to get such a friendly welcome. The explanation came when a white work truck, packed with a Navajo family, pulled over to talk to us one afternoon. They were so excited to see us and were smiling as they rolled down the window.

"You're the people who are walking across America, right?" they asked with a distinctly Navajo accent. "We saw you and just had to stop."

It seems a Navajo Christian radio station in Window Rock, AZ had picked up on our story somehow and had been talking about us since the beginning of the walk. That's why so many Navajos had been waving at us. They knew who we were and what we were doing! I still believe those prayers of confession, asking God to break down the walls of division between us and the Native American people, paid great dividends throughout the walk and even after. We would see this happen repeatedly as God gave us special favor with the Native American people.

There were very few times on the walk when we were truly scared. I think I can safely say we never felt threatened by people. Dogs…now that's a different story. In the more remote parts of the Navajo reservation, back on dirt roads out of sight of the Interstate, packs of dogs were common. Before the walk began, we had been warned by other cross-country walkers that dogs would be a major problem. They were right. On Tuesday morning, we started our walk on one of these roads. It was a very rough dirt road we had scouted out the prior evening. We noticed then there were quite a few dogs that looked wild. As a matter of fact, this whole section of back road looked a bit rough. We had had to find an alternative to the Interstate because of a huge gorge that was spanned by a very long bridge with no shoulder. There was no safe way to cross the Interstate bridge, so we were forced to look for another route. We hadn't walked long before we saw a pack of dogs headed right for us. We crossed to the other side of the road hoping the dogs wouldn't see us, but they did and started to follow us. We kept walking, looking back occasionally to see where the dogs were. The second or third time we looked back, a man was calling the dogs back. We don't know where he came from, but the dogs turned around and left. A little later, another pack of dogs and then another man appeared in the middle of the pack and led them in another direction. It was the oddest thing. We both had such a sense of peace each time the man appeared. Jane thinks they were angels. I'm sure they were.

We finally got back to the access road to I-40, which in many cases is just old 66. We met our drivers at a tourist stop, one of the few remnants of Route 66's glory days. We met Kit Monroe, one of the few non-Navajo encounters of the week. Kit was a truck driver who had pulled into the parking lot of old Route 66 store where tourists were looking for souvenirs. He saw the signs on our van and wanted to know more about the walk. We shared with him a little and he gave us two dollars to help with the walk. We never asked for money, but from time to time someone would give us a few dollars. Jane always put that money back in a special place to give away when we met people in need. It was amazing how many times the money that accumulated in Jane's waist pack was exactly what was needed to meet someone's need later.

We were on the verge of more milestones. Just outside of Gallup, New Mexico, we passed the one-quarter of the way point. It was hard to believe, but we had already walked over 700 miles. Physically we were tired each night, but we were becoming accustomed to the physical drain. The biggest physical challenge continued to be Jane's feet. She had been fighting horrible blisters since the second week. Nothing she tried kept her from getting them, but she had learned to manage them after they appeared. Now she had a new problem. The big toe on her left foot had become infected under the nail. It was terribly painful, even at night when she got into bed. Just the sheets touching it would bring tears to her eyes. You can imagine how it hurt to put shoes and socks on and walk twenty miles. Our drivers, Ron and Betty, encouraged her to go to the doctor and even offered to pay, but Jane chose to wait. I think she was afraid the doctor would tell her to stay off her feet for a few days or maybe even more. She knew that would put us far behind on our schedule. She continued walking and eventually, the infection got better. She did, however, lose the nail which brought challenges of its own.

As we crossed the one-fourth mark, we were also getting ready for another milestone…our fourth state, New Mexico. The mesas, buttes, and rocky cliffs were breathtaking. Just about the time you thought you'd seen the most beautiful thing you could imagine, something around the next bend would surpass it. But the one thing that thrilled us almost as much as the beauty of creation was walking up to a new state sign. With every "Welcome to …" sign, came a fresh release of faith we could indeed walk across America. Entering New Mexico was no exception, and we were thrilled to be only one day's walk from Gallup.

As we approached Gallup, we could see the truck stop a half-mile or so down the road. Our drivers were waiting there for us and we were anxious to reach the van so we could sit down for a while and rest before walking into town. Just then, Jane and I noticed a sign which read "Twin Buttes Nazarene Church." Just past the sign was a large gravel parking lot with a few trucks parked in front of the modest church building. There were four men positioned at various heights on the scaffolding erected in front of the building.

We did not walk past many church buildings on the first fourth of our walk. Whenever we did, we tried to stop and at least leave a card. If there was noticeable activity at the building, we would go in and say hello. Here was the perfect opportunity to share with some folks about the walk and perhaps even fellowship for a few minutes with some believers. So even though we were tired and ready for some rest, we decided to stop in and chat.

As we approached the building, it became apparent the workers were Navajo. By the time we got to the building, one of the workers had come down to meet us (This man later told us that when two white people walk up it usually means trouble. He thought we might be building inspectors). We introduced ourselves and asked if the pastor was around. We were told that the pastor, Wilkinson Sage, was up on the scaffold. We waved up at the pastor and soon he, along with the others, were on their way down to meet us as well.

Jane was wearing her Oklahoma Baptist University hooded sweatshirt that day and the first man who met us had noticed it. It turned out he had been to OBU for a Native American conference and his son had been recruited by OBU to play basketball. The connection to OBU opened the door for us to share our hearts with these men. Despite the justifiable suspicion these men may have had, God had ordered our steps, directed our paths and even chosen Jane's outfit, enabling us to have this opportunity. The longer we shared the friendlier they became, and our spirits began to identify with each other. Soon they were going to their trucks for cameras. They all wanted their pictures taken with us. It was wonderful.

All this time, our drivers were waiting a few blocks down the road. By this time, we were forty-five minutes late arriving. Our walking speed was very consistent, and we could usually predict our arrival time at the support vehicle within just a few minutes. We didn't know it, but they had begun to worry.

While they worried, we were snapping picture after picture with our new friends at the Navajo church. We began saying our goodbyes and then something happened we hadn't expected.

"What are you doing tonight?" they asked, almost in unison.

You must remember, most mornings we got up at 4 a.m. We spent about three hours getting prepared and ready to walk by having our quiet times, making lunches, eating breakfast and getting dressed for the day. Then we walked for eight to ten hours, fixed supper when we got home, and doctored our aching bodies from a long hard day. Not surprisingly, we were planning on doing that night what we did every other night. We were going to rest and go to bed!

"What did you have in mind?" we asked, not really wanting an answer.

"We're having revival service tonight and we'd like you to come and share your story with our people," the pastor said.

Jane and I looked at each other. We knew from experience that Navajo services could last several hours. It didn't begin until 7 p.m. We had been going to bed at 8:30 p.m. We looked at each other and knew we shouldn't do it. But we also knew the commitment we had made to the Lord long ago; we would walk through whatever doors He opened. Yes, was the only answer we could give. Yes, was the answer we gave.

We arranged with the pastor and his friends to share our story near the beginning of the service and then slip out. The service was scheduled to begin at 7 p.m. but our previous experience with Navajo churches, and many other churches for that matter, told us it would probably be later. However, when we pulled into the parking lot a few minutes before 7, we could already hear the singing. They had started early.

During our visit earlier that day, we had been given a tour of the newly remodeled building. They were so proud of their building and especially of their 144 new white plastic chairs. When we arrived, nearly every chair was filled, and people were still pulling into the parking lot. The people were obviously expecting us because as soon as we walked through the door, the Navajos began to greet us and then ushered Jane and I and our two drivers right down front to seats of honor. We were the only white people in the entire building.

True to his word, not long after the service started, our new friend got up to introduce us. Although he was speaking Navajo, we knew he was talking about us because he held up one of our brochures as he spoke. Soon he motioned for us to come to the stage and speak to the crowd of people who had gathered. There are simply no words to describe the emotion which flooded our hearts as we stood facing the sea of dark-skinned Navajos. Every eye was on us as I tried to get out the first words. I choked on the emotion, afraid to cry because I wasn't sure if they would understand why. Somehow, I managed to get out an introduction and shared about how God had broken our hearts for our nation. Whenever I looked out over the congregation, more emotion made its way up from my heart to the lump in my throat. Why did these people move me so? Why was my heart aching and rejoicing at the same time? For some reason, which I could not explain, I felt strangely connected to these Navajos and all the other people we had met along the streets and sidewalks of our nation. I believed it went back to those prayers when we asked for the heart and eyes of Jesus. For the first time in my life, I felt I was identifying with the tears Jesus shed over His Jerusalem. This nation we were walking through had become my Jerusalem.

When we finished sharing with the congregation, they clapped. As we left the stage and went back to our seats, we could see tears rolling down many Navajo faces. When we left a little while later, we shook hands and exchanged smiles all the way to the back door. I could not help but picture our common Father looking down and smiling. He was observing something He sees far too infrequently; His children acting like His children. Our hearts were full to overflowing as we drove away. Once again, we resolved to be an example of Jesus' unconditional love as we took each step. And…so we walked.

Chapter 12

There were days when we walked all day, twenty miles or more, and never saw a single person. There were many days, especially in the desert, when we spoke to only one or two people during the day. We would then walk into a city like Gallup, New Mexico, where there were people everywhere and encounters happened one after another, almost too quickly. I cannot accurately convey what it's like to have spiritual conversations with people in rapid-fire succession. It's exhilarating and exhausting at the same time. We were not just exchanging cordial greetings or pleasantries. Instead, we saw every encounter as a divine appointment that could have eternal consequences. We were trying to be respectful as we listened, aware of people's physical and emotional needs as we shared, and sensitive to God's nudging as we spoke tenderly yet honestly about Jesus. All of this we tried to do while holding our conversations to a few minutes in length. During the three hour-walk through Gallup, we had numerous encounters. There were too many to recount, but this is a sampling of that afternoon.

Thomas Murphy, a Navajo, was walking along Route 66 just west of town. He was trying to get a ride back to Sanders, Arizona. A few minutes later, another Navajo, Raymond Murphy, was looking for his brother Thomas. Both men had been drinking but were sober enough to hear and understand the gospel.

As we approached the street corner, the "Don't Walk" sign started flashing. Jane said, "There must be a reason we were stopped here." Immediately we were approached by a Navajo man whom Jane recognized from lunch. He had come through the restaurant trying to sell his hand-made jewelry. Brian had a black eye and horrible bruises all over his arms and body. He had been mugged, beaten and robbed of all his earnings the day before. He was penniless and homeless. He had been given temporary housing in an old run-down hotel around the corner. His children were there waiting for their father to make enough money to buy them lunch. We shared the gospel with Brian. We purchased an inexpensive bracelet to help him. We got in a circle there on Route 66 and prayed for him. We cried. We listened to the familiar story of how he had been taken from his family at an early age to Salt Lake City for "education"; the kind where his mouth was washed out with soap for speaking Navajo. Our hearts broke. We cried again. We walked on.

Jane slipped into a Taco Bell to use the restroom. While inside, she shared the gospel with an employee. Outside I was talking to George, the only Zuni I would share with on the entire walk. George had a bad knee and had been going to the medicine man for help. His knee was only getting worse. I asked George if he'd heard of Jesus, the Great Healer. He had. I shared the gospel in detail with George. I asked him if he would ask Jesus into his heart. He cried but could not, not yet. As tears rolled down his weathered red cheeks, I asked him if I could pray for him to be healed. He said yes. When I was done praying, George was still crying. I asked him to remember my prayer. I told him when his knee got better to give God all the glory, not the medicine man. He promised he would. We walked on.

There was a DHL delivery truck parked outside a business as we approached another corner. The female delivery person came out the door and down the steps just as we walked by. Another divine appointment? Yes. The delivery person had seen us four times that day as we walked through Gallup. This made an impression on her, and she wanted to know all about the walk. We shared with her, asked if she knew Jesus, which she did, and then smiled and shook her hand as we left. It wasn't until later that week we learned the impact God had allowed us to make on her life. We received this email a few days later.

"Hi! I met you in Gallup a couple of days ago as you were walking through the city. I just want you to know how much it meant to me that you stopped and talked. In my work people can be very rude and impatient. It seems I can never do enough to please people. It's very frustrating. The other day when your wife smiled and you two took time to talk with me it just...well it kind of restored my faith in mankind. Just wanted you to know. God Bless."

The DHL Lady

We have emailed back and forth several times with Joni, the DHL lady since then. Just a few words and a smile made a big difference. When people ask us if we think the walk made any difference, we both look at each other and think of the DHL lady.

Next, it was Dean, a young, nicely dressed Navajo who was walking in our direction. His car was in the shop, so he was walking home. We walked alongside him and shared. Then it was Benny, an older Navajo who stopped us on the street. He wanted to know what we were doing, and we told him. Then two Navajo men flagged us down as we passed a parking lot. They were leaning against the outside of a store and had been drinking. We told them what we were doing, and the more outspoken of the two said he wanted to walk to Washington D.C. with us. Imagine the kind of problem this would have presented. Here we had an intoxicated Navajo and his buddy who, at the drop of a hat, wanted to join us as we walked. As we talked, we found out they were homeless and had spent the night before in the ditch. They would probably do the same that night. They wanted to go home with us and get up tomorrow morning to walk.

As they walked alongside us, we learned our new friend's name was Kasmira, which he said meant "the bad one." He explained he felt because of his name, he could only be bad. Others had told him all his life he was bad. I just could not let this go, so I asked Kasmira if he would mind if I gave him a new name. He readily agreed. I had noticed Kasmira walked with a slight limp, so I told him his new name would be Jacob. We told him the story of Jacob as we walked along, and he was thrilled to have a "good name". We arranged to meet Jacob the next morning at that spot if he was determined to walk with us. He agreed, but the next morning he was not there.

This story illustrates the adventurous aspect of the walk we faced every day. When the day began, we had no intention of taking on a sidekick. However, as soon as we met Jacob, we had to be open to the possibility that perhaps this was what God wanted. We didn't know from one day to the next what God was going to do and how He would choose to bring people into our lives. Having Jacob join us wasn't what we would have chosen for ourselves, but we had to have willing hearts. It kept us on our toes for sure.

A couple of other interesting side notes about that afternoon in Gallup, NM. One, when Jane and I got done walking, we had to wait for our drivers to come to pick us up. This was very unusual. Most of the time our drivers were waiting for us with bottles of cold water and were as anxious as we were to get back and get some rest. But on this day, I had to call to find out where our drivers were. Their response amazed me. They said the van was surrounded by people asking questions and just as soon as they could deal with all the people and share what they felt God wanted them to share, they'd come to get us. It still makes me laugh to think about it.

The second interesting thing was we ended our walk at a Muslim mosque. It was the only time this happened. We did see other mosques, but on this day, it was right there. Jane and I wrestled some with how to pray when we passed places like a mosque or a place of worship where people were being taught belief systems that turned them away from the Truth. I'm not referring to different denominations or a church that may vary slightly from what we believe. We walked by hundreds of Christian churches where we felt very good about praying for God's blessing, growth, unity, the church leadership and continued spiritual maturity. However, when we walked by places where we truly believed the error being taught was greater than any truth, we prayed differently. Understand, we did not pray for bad things to happen, for their buildings to burn down, or for their leaders to die. We prayed God would bind the spirit of deception and confusion and release the Spirit of truth. We prayed their eyes would be opened, not to our truth, but His truth, and they would begin seeing Jesus for who He really is. We also prayed other followers of Jesus would be loving and representatives of Jesus' compassionate nature when dealing with them.

The need for this type of prayer crystallized in Gallup, NM. A couple of days earlier, we had pulled into our campground for the week. We had chosen this campground in part because the advertisement stated the park was owned by a veteran. We tried to patronize businesses owned by vets and do whatever else we could along the walk to show our appreciation for these men and women who had sacrificed immensely to serve our country. As we pulled into the campground, we started noticing the pro-American signs along the driveway. The further down the drive we went, the more anti-Muslim the signs became. When we began the check-in procedure, the owner began telling us about the other campground in town which was owned by Muslims. The conversation went downhill from there. God began teaching us that day that being patriotic doesn't mean being anti-something, or more importantly, anti-someone else. Being a Christian doesn't either. We have done a lot of damage by conveying to the rest of the world that being a Christian means you hate everyone who isn't. Nothing could be further from the truth. No attitude could hurt the cause of Christ as much as this one. That attitude and sentiment are much more common than you'd think and infinitely more common than it should be in the Church. It made us wish we had camped at the campground owned by Muslims. The truth was: Every day we walked; we were learning. God was teaching us. And…so we walked.

Chapter 13

Most of the time the walk was about people. It was about praying with people, feeding people, sharing God's love and purpose with people, and discovering just how wonderful most people really are. And then there were other times when it became more about walking than about anything else.

That is not to say the walking didn't have spiritual significance, because it did. The idea of walking across America had come directly from the scriptural principle in Joshua 1:3. We both felt compelled to put down the soles of our feet, from one side of the country to the other, every step of the way. The commitment to complete that task, when the road became difficult for one reason or another, required more courage, strength, and more love for one another than we had ever needed before in our lives.

A lot of times when you look back at challenging times in your life, you realize they weren't as hard as you thought. But when it comes to the difficult times we endured during the walk across America, looking back now doesn't diminish the intensity at all. If anything, we look back and say how in the world did we do that?

One such day occurred just east of Rehoboth, New Mexico. Once again, we had run out of old Route 66. We stopped by the Highway Patrol station to get permission to walk on the Interstate, but the officer in charge wouldn't give his blessing. We asked if there were any other side roads that would get us to Continental Divide, New Mexico, where 66 began again. He knew of nothing. Our drivers had gone exploring in the morning to find an alternate route. When we met them for lunch, they broke the bad news; we would have to walk nine miles that afternoon on the railroad tracks.

There were two challenges for the afternoon walk. One, the weather was cold and breezy. The morning had begun with one of the lowest temperatures of the walk, 5 degrees with a much colder wind chill. Now, in the middle of the day, the temperature hovered around 32 degrees. The sky was grey and even in the middle of the desert, it looked like winter. Two, since there were no access points along the tracks, there would be nowhere to meet our drivers for a break, change socks and shoes, or rendezvous if there was an emergency.

Had we been twenty years old, these issues would only have been only a minor inconvenience. However, for two people in their fifties, with no way of protecting themselves, no communication for three or four hours, walking among mountains and buttes, and along the edge of the Navajo Reservation, this was a daunting task. It was one of those times when others we knew who had made cross-country walks would have simply gotten in a car and driven to the next section of Route 66, but we had committed and committed to walking every step of the way.

We gathered up the things we believed would best prepare us for the afternoon. We needed our trail shoes for walking on the tracks, some additional clothing for the cold weather and rain gear in case of wet snow. We also took extra socks and supplies for Jane's feet. We had two-way radios, although their range was only a mile or so. We also had our cell phones, but cell towers were few and far between this far off the Interstate. We packed extra water and snacks to sustain us for a nine-mile hike. Loaded down and already tired from the morning, we headed out on what would be one of the most challenging afternoons of the entire walk.

We started out walking along the railroad tracks but about 100 yards down the tracks the narrow service road ended. We climbed a mound of volcanic-looking rocks onto the tracks and tried walking on the railroad ties for half a mile or so. It's hard to imagine how hard it was to walk between the tracks. They were spaced in such a way that it required either very small steps to put your foot on each one or very long steps to skip a tie in between steps. Either way, it was impossible to walk with a normal stride.

We noticed a crude, red dirt road that ran parallel to the tracks. We didn't know how far it would go, but it had to be better than walking on the tracks. We climbed the barbed wire fence and onto the road. We were in the middle of the desert, many miles from a town of any significant size, on a deserted, primitive road and then, for the first time, except for a few stray flakes back in Arizona, it started to snow. It snowed large, wet, cold flakes that melted as soon as they hit the ground. Snow that melts is usually good, but not in this situation.

For one thing, the snow was melting on our bodies, making us wet. We got out our rain gear and put it on over our winter clothing because the camera, radios, and phones were getting wet. The melting snow was also turning the red clay into thick mud, which began accumulating on the bottoms of our shoes. The trail shoes we were wearing were already twice as heavy as our normal walking shoes. The soles have an all-terrain look, filled with lots of nooks and crannies for mud to get stuck. With every step we took, the red goo got thicker, and the shoes got heavier. At first, we thought it was funny and laughed as we got an inch taller with every step, but not for long. After half a dozen inches had accumulated on the bottom of the shoes, it would fall off one shoe, leaving us lopsided.

All this had happened in the first hour of the afternoon and by now the laughing had stopped. We had lost all communication with our drivers. We were wet, tired and perhaps a bit scared. We had only seen a few cars or trucks pass on the dirt road but decided to try to flag one of them down and verify we were walking on a road that was going to get us where we needed to go. For the next few minutes, we tried unsuccessfully to get a few pick-up trucks to stop. We surmised the drivers were probably wondering what two people were doing walking through the backside of the desert in a snowstorm. To be perfectly honest, I was wondering exactly the same thing.

Finally, a truck slowed down and stopped. We explained to the Navajo man driving that we were lost and needed some help. He was not talkative and gave us some vague directions, pointing us in the general direction we were already walking. It was clear our presence made him uncomfortable. He put the truck in gear to pull away and I quickly handed him one of our cards. Just down the road, we began to make out the outline of a few houses through the falling snow. It was a small group of maybe ten or twelve, newer, modest ranch houses. As we passed the last one, a man came out of the front door and walked toward us. It was the man who had reluctantly stopped down the road. He was holding the card I had given him in his hand, reading it as he walked.

"Are you really walking across America?" he asked.

We assured him we were. He seemed a little puzzled as to how we had gotten to where we were. His expression told me he didn't think this was the right road to be on to walk across America.

We talked with our new Navajo friend Ray for a few minutes before getting down to the most key issue.

"Ray, we're walking across America to tell people about Jesus. Do you know him?" I asked.

What happened in that split second occurred hundreds of times across America. The name "Jesus" caused an immediate reaction. This time it was positive. Ray smiled and then looked a little embarrassed.

He said he was a Christian, told us the name of the church he attended, and began giving us explicit directions on how to proceed, without us having to ask again. It's a good thing he did too. The dirt road through the desert took several twists and turns and the railroad track was about to split in two different directions. Had we taken the wrong turn we could have been lost for days in the desert.

I learned an important lesson that day. I think Ray did too. I learned what makes us the same ought to be much stronger than what makes us different. I knew this truth, at least in theory most of my life, but it takes on a whole new meaning when you are lost in the New Mexico desert. Since leaving Santa Monica pier, we had encountered hundreds, perhaps thousands of people, with whom we had little in common. We could have become calloused to the differences and not allowed them to change our hearts. Instead, we committed ourselves to a higher standard of love and acceptance. We purposefully routed ourselves through areas where God could stretch us to become more like Jesus. With each step we took through inner cities, homeless tent camps, reservations and opulent neighborhoods, we were able to sense God melting away what we perceived as differences. We knew every time we put down the soles of our feet, we were reclaiming a piece of our hearts that had been stolen by preconceived notions and judgment. We knew we were being healed from the inside out, with every footstep. We wanted that kind of healing for our nation too. And…so we walked.

Chapter 14

The rest of that afternoon in the desert was nothing short of unbelievable. When we left Ray, we followed his directions exactly. The path he had laid out for us went across cattle crossings, gullies, and back and forth across barbed wire fences that separated the road from the railroad tracks. It snowed all afternoon. The mud on our shoes was almost unbearable, so we kept going back to the railroad tracks to scrape our shoes off and walk for a while where there was no mud. That is, until a train would come. We would then scurry down the gravel mound and back into the mud where we would be walking like Frankenstein within a few steps. Jane would laugh for a while, calling herself "Frank" and then almost cry. Then, in true form, she would break into song. Her singing kept us both going more than a few times.

Occasionally we would get a tower or two on the cell phone and call our drivers. We could talk for only a few moments before losing the signal. We did two things during those conversations. The first was to convey to Ron and Betty the seriousness of our situation. We were walking at a crawl because of the weather and looking for the landmarks Ray had given us. We were quickly losing daylight. We had yet to walk in the dark of night and certainly didn't want this to be the first time. The Second was to give them an indication of where we were. We looked for cell towers, mountains or anything we might both be able to see to determine how far we were apart. Nothing worked.

Then, I had an idea. We had some battery-powered strobe lights which were supposed to be visible from a couple of miles away. During our next short conversation, I asked them to get to one of the railroad crossings and sit on the tracks. I would go to the highest point I could find and start the strobe lights. If they could look in our direction up the tracks and see the light, we'd know they were close. They tried, but it didn't work. They couldn't see us at all.

By this time, I was slightly apprehensive. Although I hadn't mentioned it to Jane, I had seen several tracks in the mud which looked like coyote tracks. A few were larger and more cat-like, probably from mountain lions that came down at night to feed. I had already begun looking at the small railroad overpasses as potential shelters for the night. I didn't like our chances if we were truly lost from the drivers until daybreak. The wet snow had soaked our clothes. Our feet were wet, and our shoes were caked with mud. We did not have our extreme cold-weather gear and had precious little water and food. The temperature by morning would be near zero in the desert. Exhaustion was imminent.

The phone rang. I was sure it was the drivers saying they had spotted us. Instead, it was our daughter Rebekah. She called faithfully most every afternoon to check on us. The call itself was a miracle since we had only been able to connect with our drivers for a few moments at a time. This connection was clear and lasted for several minutes. I quickly apprised her of our situation and told her my makeshift plans; should we be forced to wait for our driver's arrival after dark. Jane could overhear the conversation and was hearing all my fears for the first time. She kept turning around and looking at me as if she couldn't believe what she was hearing. Jane seldom allows herself to go down negative mental pathways. She always assumes things will turn out well and that positive attitude generally serves her well. But she knew because we were so tired, and it was getting dark so quickly, there was a small chance we were in trouble.

"Daddy," Rebekah said, "I want to share with you the Bible verse I've been memorizing this week. It's Exodus 23:20. It says, 'See, I am sending an angel ahead of you to guard you along the way and to bring you to the place I have prepared.' Daddy, you're going to be alright. God will bring you safely to the right place."

Just then, while still talking to Rebekah, our drivers drove by, going the opposite direction, on the little red dirt road on the north side of the barbed-wire fence. We started yelling and screaming but they didn't hear us and kept on driving. After thanking her for her encouragement, I hung up with Rebekah, then quickly called the drivers to tell them to turn around and pick us up. By the time they got back to us, we had climbed the fence and were waiting for them beside the road. They were relieved, but not as relieved as Jane and me. As we cleaned the mud off our shoes, we realized we were muddy up to our knees. We took off our dirty shoes and climbed into the van just as the last minutes of daylight slipped behind the buttes.

The ride back to Gallup was a strange one. I wanted to talk about the afternoon, but I couldn't. I was thinking about the "what ifs". What if Ray hadn't changed his mind about giving us detailed directions? What if we hadn't seen the van drive by? What if we had had to spend the night in the cold desert? I realized for the first time during the walk how close we had come to real danger. Lots of other times had been painful and inconvenient, but this was the first time I realized the potential for life and death kind of danger. Without being an alarmist, I believe this day could have ended in tragedy had it not been for the One who was watching over us.

This day had been intense and pivotal in a very important way. Up until this point I dealt with the possible dangers of the walk by simply dismissing them. But on this day, the combination of wet weather, below-freezing temperatures, less than adequate provisions, communication devices that did not work, and the lack of knowledge of where we were walking was enough to jolt me into this reality: this walk had the potential to take our lives. This did not mean fear would rule the day from this point forward. It did mean however, we would approach each day's walk with caution over the next several months. We never doubted our call or God's presence. But we did begin to realize God would allow us to confront real dangers from time to time, reminding us that obedience is most often accompanied by a price tag and requires a prerequisite of faith.

We had plans to meet with our dear friends, Freddy and Nancy Hall, missionaries to the Navajos, in Gallup for dinner. Over the years we had been on several summer mission trips to the Navajo Nation in Shiprock, New Mexico to work with the Navajo children at their church. They had kept up with us during the walk, offered invaluable advice on walking in and around the Navajo Reservation, and made us promise we'd meet them when we got close. We were late getting back to town so there was no time to clean up. We arrived at the restaurant covered in mud and so tired we could barely walk. After eating, sharing about our day and recounting many of our experiences on the walk thus far, we were refreshed. Being with good friends always had a way of encouraging us on this journey. We snapped a few pictures, said our goodbyes, and as we had done so many times along the way, got in a circle and prayed with those who cared for us.

Saturday morning, we went back to the spot where our drivers had found us the night before and started walking east. The sun was out, it was warm, and the mud had dried overnight. We walked a few miles along the railroad tracks and then up past some buildings into Continental Divide, New Mexico, where Route 66 began again. We would never again take a paved road to walk on, for granted.

Five more miles down Old 66 was Thoreau, New Mexico. Our week ended much as it had begun, at an old "mother road" trading post. This one had been out of business for years, from the look of it. We had now crossed the Continental Divide and the tallest of the mountains were behind us, as were California, Nevada and Arizona. We had walked over 755 miles in seven weeks. We had met hundreds of people, told the story of Jesus more times than we could count, and learned to depend on God more than we ever thought possible. I had a new appreciation for our Lord, The Sustainer, and had come to love my wife at a depth I could have never imagined before the walk. We were changed in ways that made us stronger emotionally, spiritually and physically. We were experiencing a transformation in our lives day by day which I believe could have only happened while being obedient to do something as radical as walking across America. We were aware of the changes and so were others. They were changes for the better. Changes that made us more like our Savior. Changes that seemed to come one step at a time. And…so we walked.

Chapter 15

On Monday morning we began walking in Thoreau, New Mexico. We were going to be walking along I-40 on an old, nearly deserted section of Route 66. That usually meant limited interaction with people. As we had our daily prayer at the starting point for the day, I prayed this prayer:

"Lord, do whatever you have to in our lives and in the daily events of others in order to make sure our paths intersect. Do whatever it takes to allow us the opportunity to share Your love with those who need to hear about it today."

I felt very strongly about it and prayed that prayer with real conviction. I knew there were those who needed to hear the gospel that very day. We had been walking for about 10 minutes when we saw a car stopped on the shoulder ahead of us. As we got closer, we could see a woman, probably in her sixties, down off the road among the tumbleweeds and cacti, retrieving her tire. It had fallen off as she started to get on the Interstate. I ran down into the field and carried up the tire. When I got to the car, I saw that not only had the tire and wheel come off, but the brake mechanism had fallen off the axle and was lying on the pavement. My mind was already racing, trying to figure out how I was going to turn this into a sharing opportunity. The woman remarked she was glad this didn't happen on the Interstate going 75 miles per hour. I replied, "The Lord must have really been looking out for you," to which she replied, "I guess *she* was." My first thought was, "What have we gotten ourselves into." As I propped the tire up against the back of her car, I saw her bumper sticker which declared her religion of choice was Wicca and that she was a practicing witch!

Our driver had already driven ahead three miles, leaving us alone and feeling a little vulnerable. We'd already mentioned to Barbara, the stranded witch, we were walking across America. Before we could figure out what to do next, she asked, "Why are you walking across America?" Without missing a beat or blinking an eye, I blurted out we were walking across America to tell people about Jesus. As the words were coming out of my mouth, I was thinking, "Why are you saying this to a witch?" I just kept talking and the more I talked, the bolder I got. I figured I might as well get it in while I could. After all, she wasn't going anywhere because her tire and wheel were laying there on the ground! Then Jane got in on the conversation and said, "God must have really wanted you to hear how much He loves you." We were like a tag team, giving her the gospel from both sides. She was most likely wishing she really could just evaporate into thin air. I continued, "You know, you are an answer to prayer. As a matter of fact, you are the first answer to a prayer I prayed just ten minutes ago." I explained to her what I had just prayed. "I'm very sorry God made the tire and wheel fall off your car so you could be here at just the right time. I'm sorry for your inconvenience and we will do whatever we can to help you get your car fixed, but I'm telling you, God loves you so much He went to all this trouble to cause your path to intersect ours this morning, so you could hear what we've got to say."

Although it sounds almost humorous, it was anything but funny then. We offered to make a call for her, to put her in touch with some Christian mechanics we had met the day before, or to help her get a tow. We did what we could to share the gospel with her and told her we'd be praying for her. Jane and I walked off down the road rejoicing for such an awesome opportunity to share the gospel. As we walked, we rebuked the enemy and prayed for protection over ourselves and our families. We knew the enemy was not happy about what had just happened and would certainly not hesitate to unleash the powers of darkness against us and the walk. We prayed for protection diligently regarding this encounter for weeks and still pray for God's hedge to be about us whenever we think of this day. We thank God for the promise; "greater is He who is in us than He that is in the world".

As we continued down the road toward Grants, New Mexico, we met Nate and Lewis, two Native Americans. They were walking from Grants, out several miles to their home and so took a special interest in the fact we were walking across America. We took a long time to talk and share with them. Like so many others we talked to, they had been exposed to religious cults which caused them to be skeptical of Christians. We gave them our card, prayed with them and parted ways.

On Tuesday, Pastor Hugh Rogers from First Baptist Church in Grants walked with us. Pastor Hugh showed up to walk that morning in his cowboy hat and leather boots. I wondered how long he would last in those boots. He was determined and walked nine miles right alongside us. Our first encounter of the day was a pair of familiar faces. Nate and Lewis were walking home again. This time they had been drinking. Nate was belligerent and argumentative. We split them up, so Jane and Pastor Hugh could talk with Lewis, while I talked with Nate. He was up for a fight, and although I never felt threatened, I'm also not sure I did much good. Jane and Pastor Hugh seemed to make some headway with Lewis and as always, our prayer was for God to use our conversations to show His love.

A little further up the road, we saw a small outreach mission. Inside I met Fernando, not the pastor, but a worker in the church. He was of Hispanic/Native American heritage and his English was limited, broken, and extremely difficult to understand through the thick accent. After I shared with him about who we were and about our walk across America, he began telling me his story. He said God had called him to walk from New Mexico to Florida, sharing Christ with Spanish-speaking Americans. He had been hesitant to say yes to God, not knowing how he would be able to make the trip on foot. When I shared with him that Jane and I had already walked nearly 800 miles he got a big smile on his face, as if to say, "If you can do it, I can do it." I prayed with Fernando before I left and asked God to bless his journey. One of the things God had asked us to do was to encourage others in their walk. I have often wondered about Fernando and others like him who were encouraged to say yes to their calling, because of our obedience. I hope someday in eternity we will get to meet all of those who were directly or indirectly affected by the walk.

As we left the little mission, we saw a white pickup truck across the street. The truck belonged to the sanitation department and the men had just gotten out of the truck to begin loading a big pile of white trash bags into the back. We ran across the street and I asked the men if they'd mind if I loaded the trash. This had to be God because I had no interest in picking up trash. This was one of those times I felt supernaturally empowered to do and say things that accomplished His purpose. The sanitation workers, Elias and Louis, didn't mind, so I began throwing the bags into the truck. I talked with them about Jesus and how He had asked us to be helpful servants to all men. I thanked them for the opportunity to serve them and shared the gospel with them before they left. I felt strangely alive and knew what had just happened was something extremely powerful and rare. At that moment, I understood, as never before, what it meant for Christ to live in and through me. It was one of the most personally profound moments on the entire walk for me. Who could imagine throwing some trash bags around could be so spiritual?

As we entered Grants, there were too many encounters to count. There were hitchhikers, walkers, homeless, and people sitting in cars. Many were just standing or sitting seemingly waiting for us to arrive. Whenever other people walked with us in their own hometown, they were amazed at the number of people who were right in front of them every day who needed love and companionship.

We arrived at the rescue mission in downtown Grants just in time for the lunch meal to be served. It was another awesome experience. I was asked to pray before the meal and then we began moving around the room, meeting and talking with people. One of the men waiting for a meal was Juan. This elderly man in his eighties comes every day for a free lunch. He is a veteran of World War II, an increasingly rare breed these days. He was so thankful we took time to speak with him. We thanked him for his service to our country.

Juan represents an ever-growing segment of our population... the elderly. This was one of the things which made a lasting impression on Jane and me as we walked. Everywhere we went there were older Americans sitting in coffee shops, doughnut shops, on park benches, and even living on the streets. Medical science and the availability of healthcare have helped senior adults live longer. They now make up a larger percentage of our population than could have ever been foreseen just a few generations ago. These increasing numbers of elderly Americans, find themselves dealing with age-related difficulties alone. Many families have abandoned their grandparents and great-grandparents. Many are isolated with practically no human interaction. Unfortunately, the Church has not done enough to minister to these dear folks. There are vast numbers of elderly who are living with little or no spiritual influence in their life at a time when they need it more than ever. Those, like Juan, are now facing death and eternity. They have time to consider spirituality, and most would welcome the opportunity to begin a relationship with Christ if someone would lovingly sow into their lives.

As the week progressed, we were privileged to walk through several more Native American reservations. The homelands of the Laguna and Acoma tribes were our first since the Navajo Nation. Here we were attacked by a wolf-dog hybrid. It was a very bad place to find out the tear gas spray I had been carrying since the beginning of the walk didn't work. Fortunately, a flurry of cars passing by frightened the animal off, but it was frightening enough to make me see stars for a few minutes.

We made a wonderful discovery as we walked through these reservations and realized each tribe had a unique and distinguishing physical appearance. In typical Caucasian naiveté we didn't think about different tribes looking differently, but after observing the Navajos for hundreds of miles we were amazed at how the appearance of the Laguna and Acoma people was unique. We noticed the same thing as we walked across Pueblo land. Although our personal interaction with these tribes was limited, we used the long hours of walking through a beautiful land strewn with Pueblo ruins to pray for these incredibly talented and resourceful people. There were many

Christian churches along the way which received our blessings and prayers as well.

One of the most disturbing things we were made aware of as we walked through areas heavily populated by Native Americans is how condescending some people can be toward those who were here first. On Wednesday morning we were walking along Old 66 when Jane spotted a woman named Mary out in her yard. She had moved to this area from back East, to start a touristy-type business, based on the art forms of the Native Americans. Before Jane could share much about our walk, Mary told Jane about all the negatives of living near "Indians." She told Jane an unbelievable story about how one Christmas she picked up all the trash in her neighbor's yard, put it in trash bags, piled it on their porch, rang the doorbell, and told them picking up their trash was her Christmas present to them. She was serious and thought she had done something admirable. She couldn't understand why her actions had offended them.

I wondered what kind of impact Mary had on her neighbors. It led me to consider that sometimes the most poignant witness we can have is to walk prayerfully and respectfully through the lives of others. There were plenty of times we used words, conversations, and one-on-one sharing to convey the love of God. There were hundreds of other times when our most effective evangelistic tool was simple prayer as we walked past the homes of families, school buses filled with children or funeral processions lined with grieving survivors. There were other times when our mightiest spiritual weapon was respect for the ground we walked on, for the environment we were passing through, and for personal property. We tried never to throw down a piece of trash beside the road. Our desire was to never knowingly trespass or violate laws or rules. Many times, it would have been easier or more convenient and perhaps even saved us steps to cross a yard or walk against a traffic signal. We tried very hard not to. Why? First, because it's the right thing to do. The Bible is clear about the fact that part of our responsibility as Christian citizens is to live within the boundaries and limitations of the law. Second, it's important because we have been made stewards of this wonderful creation. I'm not talking about environmental extremism, just using godly judgment in how we maintain the place we have been allowed to live. And last, it's important because people are watching. They're watching to see whether our words match our deeds. They want to know if our preaching is matched by a life of integrity and authenticity.

I thought about Jesus a lot during our walk. I tried to imagine His character and how He might have behaved if He were doing something similar. I couldn't for a moment imagine Him throwing down His trash, or even worse, trash-talking the people whose land He was passing through. Jesus showed us by his example, we "talk" loudest by how we "walk". And…so we walked.

Chapter 16

By Thursday we had once again lost the paved version of Route 66. Our stacks of maps and books about the glory years of the old highway couldn't put it back the way it used to be. We were once again relegated to dirt roads far from the superhighway. It's difficult to explain what these roads are like. There are no houses, no businesses, no shoulders for the driver to pull off on, no bathrooms, and virtually no people. These characteristics are both the downside and the upside of walking these roads. They are tough miles to be sure, but they are some of the most natural and undisturbed places in the country. On Thursday we saw two small herds of wild horses grazing and then galloping through the desert. You could easily imagine the days before the Wild West, before cowboys, and before fences when these wild stallions would have raced each other from one side of the desert to the other. The sight of their manes flowing as they ran will be forever etched in our memories.

By Friday we had even run out of dirt roads. Our only option was the Interstate highway. Our driver called the Highway Patrol and got permission for us to walk on the Interstate for the nine miles between where we were and where Route 66 started up again, just west of Albuquerque. The New Mexico Highway Patrol had one unusual request. They asked that we walk with traffic and that our escort van be behind us with the emergency flashers on. We had never walked this way, as we always preferred facing traffic, and could not imagine this was safe for us or the van. But this was what they requested and so we obliged.

We saw within just a few minutes that this was going to be problematic. Jane and I started walking on the Interstate with the van sitting behind us. I had asked Stacy, our driver, to let us walk half a mile or so ahead, come up behind us, park and turn the van off. (Our old van with 150,000 miles was tired and tended to overheat when sitting and idling.) When we walked a half mile ahead again, she would repeat the process. People coming up from behind us saw a van on the shoulder, with flashers on, and then in a few seconds, they saw two people walking away from the van toward the next exit. They assumed we were having car trouble and were walking to get help. Many of them stopped to help, but by the time they saw us and pulled off onto the shoulder, they were a quarter of a mile ahead of us. We'd have to run to where they were to tell them we didn't need help. This became one more way to share the gospel. During the first few miles, we had 12 cars, 2 semis, and a Highway Patrol all stop to help. Each one of them got an explanation of why we were walking and the all-important question, "Do you know Jesus?"

We soon changed our method and had Stacy go ahead to the next exit and wait for us. It was a compromise. We were still walking with traffic but without an escort. It worked. Since the van was not on the highway, people stopped pulling over to help. The first few miles had exhausted us as we had run most of those miles. The good news? In one morning, we had set a record for the most people talked to in such a short distance.

Saturday's nine-and-a-half-mile walk would put us in the heart of Albuquerque, our largest city since Flagstaff, Arizona. This would leave only one more major city, Amarillo, Texas, before the halfway point of Oklahoma City. After Albuquerque, the elevation would drop for the next 1000 miles. This would mean easier breathing and less climbing. Albuquerque had been circled on the map in my mind for many months, but we could never have imagined all God would do there.

As we entered Albuquerque on Route 66, we noticed an antique pickup truck, in immaculate condition, pulled into a little adobe motel on our left. The little motor inn looked like a relic left over from the 1960s. The driver got out of his truck and sat on the edge of an adobe planter which still contained a few cacti. He appeared to be waiting for someone, perhaps us. The man was neatly dressed, well-groomed, and had a perfectly combed head full of jet-black hair and sparkling white teeth. His dark skin was flawless, his face cleanly shaven and his eyes were black as coal. We attempted to start a conversation with the smiling man but realized quickly he spoke no English. I pulled out one of our cards and gave it to him. He took one look at the picture of us walking on the front of the card and grinned as he looked up and said, "Jesus". The front of the card said nothing in Spanish, nothing about Jesus, and really gave no clue as to why we were walking. We smiled back and tried to find common words we could use to convey the gospel, but the only words he knew in English were "Jesus", "church", and "God." Using hand gestures, we told him our names and found out he was Juan. As we walked away, we looked back and Juan and his vintage pick-up truck were gone. We hadn't heard the door close or the engine start and now there was only an empty spot where they had been. Another angelic encounter.

Before the walk began, I had never been overly concerned with or even convinced of the physical presence of angels in this world. Perhaps, they had always been there but had gone undetected because I was not as sensitive to the supernatural as I was now. I didn't have all the answers, but I became convinced we were encountering some of God's angel army as we journeyed across our land. The longer we walked and the more angels we encountered, the more convinced we became that God had many times sent them on a mission to watch over us, encourage us and remind us that He was still affirming the walk. It never brought fear, only absolute peace and tranquility.

A few blocks down the street from Juan and his pickup, we came to a bus stop. Marlene was waiting for a city bus and so while she waited, we talked. As we began to share about Jesus, she let us know she was angry at God and had dropped out of church. She had a grandson, Toby, who was attending a Christian school down the street, and he had been trying to get her to come back to God. The more we encouraged her to renew her relationship with the Lord the less she resisted and soon we were standing at the bus stop having prayer with Marlene. When we looked up Marlene was crying. Her heart had been touched. We said our tearful goodbyes and proceeded down the street.

It was a warm sunny day in Albuquerque, especially warm for February 25th. Jane and I had shed our outerwear and were now just wearing our short-sleeved t-shirts. Those shirts were what caught the attention of Ray and Tommy as they waited near the next bus stop. Our shirts were black with the word "Worship" boldly displayed across the front. They stopped us and asked if we were Christians. When we said yes, they said they needed prayer. There on one of the main thoroughfares of Albuquerque, these two Native American men poured out their hearts to us, telling us of a failing marriage and financial hardships. We put our arms around them in a small circle and prayed. Jane had four dollars left which had been given to us by others, so she gave them each one dollar for bus fare. We waved goodbye as they stepped up onto the bus.

We were nearing the end of our week and had planned to meet some very dear friends, Scott and Cheryl Walker for lunch in the "old town" section of Albuquerque. We had been searching for the Walkers for years and God had allowed me to find them just a few days before we arrived in Albuquerque, a short drive from their home in Los Alamos. We planned to stop when we reached the Rio Grande River, but the Walkers had been slightly delayed, so we decided to walk just a couple more miles.

After crossing the Rio Grande River Bridge, we came to yet another bus stop. After so many unbelievable encounters already that day, we were tempted to just keep on walking. When I looked over at the bus stop, I saw an older African American man with weathered skin, sitting on the bench. His back was bent, and he was reading something intently. We realized every day we couldn't talk to everyone we saw. If we had, we would never have gotten any walking done. Jane usually left that decision up to me, by asking, "Yes, or no?" I always tried to be sensitive to the Holy Spirit. I looked at the man and thought, "We're almost done, we've had a great day, we need to meet our friends..." but God wouldn't let it go. I looked at Jane and said "Yes," and we walked around to the front of the bus stop.

Leslie Williams, whom it turns out was reading his Bible, was excited to meet us and to hear what we were doing. He explained he had hitchhiked from Dallas to Albuquerque to see his son, who was in jail. We had a wonderful time of praise with Leslie and I assured him that as I had approached him the Lord had spoken and said, "Tell him everything is going to be alright." As we shared with Leslie, he told us the Lord had been showing him in the Word that everything was going to be alright, and he was to be content. What confirmation! We prayed for Leslie and his son Zachary. Jane gave him her last two dollars and when we started to leave, Leslie wanted a hug from both of us. As we walked away, I wept. My heart was broken for all the hurting people who are just waiting for someone to give them a hug.

There were times along the way when I believe the Lord let me catch a "vision" of sorts. There were a few times when it was almost as though I was floating above where Jane and I were standing. It was like God was allowing me to see things from His perspective. This was one of those days. As we stood there at the bus stop with Leslie, I could see it all happening, but with an interesting twist. I saw Leslie and I saw the embrace, but it wasn't me hugging Leslie, it was Jesus. Perhaps it was on this day, for the first time it began to dawn on me that for all the walking, all the miles, the Walk to Reclaim America wasn't about the steps. It was about the stops. It wasn't so much the steps that were changing lives and making an impact, it was the stops. Our commitment to the Lord was to walk, to take the steps; that was true. But what we had learned early on and what was confirmed to us every day was this: The steps were there, not as an end to themselves, but to connect the stops together. And so, we walked…so that down the road, we would have but one more opportunity to stop.

Chapter 17

There were lots of little blessings along the way. Someone would slip us a few dollars or fill our tank up with gas. Most donations were small in comparison to the enormous cost of making a journey such as ours, but invaluable when it came to lifting our spirits and encouraging us to continue.

Such was the case on a Sunday afternoon in Moriarty, NM. We had seldom treated ourselves to our favorite foods on the walk thus far, but after walking over 800 miles we both decided we had earned a Dairy Queen Blizzard, one of Jane's top-rated indulgences. We went in and while in line to order started talking to the woman behind the counter about the walk. She got so excited when we asked her about Jesus, she could hardly contain herself. By this time Jane's Blizzard was already made but our server enthusiastically announced she'd be "super-sizing" mine, at no charge. It's hard to imagine just how much a little thing like that can mean, but believe me, those lifts came at just the right times along the way, and they carried us for miles when they happened.

On Monday morning it was back to Albuquerque to complete our walk through the city. It would take until lunchtime, about a 12-mile walk, just to get to the eastern outskirts of the metro area. During these 12 miles, we would experience a wide range of emotions from anger to sadness to sheer joy.

One of the things I expected more of than actually happened across America was disrespect for God and particularly Jesus. I had prepared myself for people who might be offended by our faith and who may even be contemptuous toward our Savior. However, even in the areas of our country where we didn't expect to find a sympathetic ear, we were confronted by very few people who wanted to argue or belittle what we were doing.

One exception happened early on Monday morning in Albuquerque. James Combs wanted to argue. He wanted to trash Jesus and he wanted to spend a lot of time doing it. Of course, he had nothing to do that day. We had 20 miles to walk. We tried to be nice. We tried to smile. The longer we talked, the more we realized James wasn't mad at Jesus. He was mad at some of His people, or at least some folks who claimed to be His. Remembering that helped me tolerate people like James a little better.

While walking across from the entrance to the campus of the University of New Mexico, we saw a young woman sitting on a bench, crying. Her head was shaved, her bohemian clothing was reminiscent of the 60s, and the distinct aroma of patchouli was thick in the air. Jane expressed our first concern as she asked, "Are you hurt?" Barely able to speak for the tears, she looked up at Jane and said, "Only in here," placing her hand on her heart. I remembered that just half a block down the road I had seen a young man walking past me with red eyes and tears rolling down his face. He had passed me so quickly I hadn't had a chance to speak with him, but now I was guessing the two had just had a fight or broken up.

I wish I had a way of letting you see how God worked through us in these kinds of situations. Jane instantly became Jesus to this young woman. She got down on her level, literally kneeling on the sidewalk and began to speak in a quiet, comforting voice. She called her name, Shannon, over and over, and told her how beautiful she was. Jane asked if she knew Jesus and when she said she had known Him long ago, Jane reminded her He still loved her and didn't want her to hurt. She asked Shannon if we might pray with her and she nodded. There, across from a university campus, with hundreds of students walking by, I joined Jane on the sidewalk beside Shannon and we prayed for God to heal her broken heart and to remind her just how much He cared for her.

A few blocks later we met Gilbert, an interesting Native American man carrying a partially carved walking stick. During our conversation, we learned he carved walking sticks to make a living. We also learned he had come as part of his morning routine, to get his medication, probably Methadone. His weathered face and fragile body told his life's story without any need for words to be spoken. He knew Jesus and so we prayed a blessing on him and on his walking stick business. I've wished many times I had had the money to buy the walking stick he was carving, as a lasting reminder of Gilbert.

Further down Central Avenue (Old 66), we went through a part of town where dozens of mobile/modular home dealers were located. We started gaining ground on an older woman walking ahead of us, and as we got closer, we could tell she was having a very difficult time walking. As we got beside her, I asked if she was in pain or if there was anything we could do for her. She was very skeptical, perhaps even a little scared at first. We told her what we were doing and told her we'd like to pray for her if we could. She was reluctant but agreed. We prayed God would ease Louise's suffering and allow her to walk without pain. We continued up the street a few blocks and stopped to eat our lunch on a little ledge beside the sidewalk. As we ate our sandwiches, Louise walked past, smiled and went on her way.

As we left the city limits and walked into the breathtaking scenery of the New Mexico desert, we saw a woman standing beside a car. She was reading a book entitled, "Chicken Soup for the Veteran". We saw this as one more opportunity to speak a word of encouragement and share our message. We met Linda Luhan, a Navy vet who spent 15 years serving our country. She had taken her grandmother's car to have some work done on the muffler but on the way home the car died and wouldn't start. We shared about all the car trouble people seemed to have when we were walking through their town and how we believed God could alter people's schedules to allow us to speak to them along the way.

We shared stories with her about people we had met and lives that had been changed through the walk. She listened with tears in her eyes and finally said, "You know, I had come to the conclusion one person couldn't make much difference. I became discouraged and just stopped trying to share my life with people because it seemed so hopeless. But after hearing some of your stories, I realize one person really can make a difference. You two have certainly made a difference in me."

Besides introducing a person to a relationship with Jesus Christ, this became our favorite response during an encounter. We realized we were walking through cities, towns, and villages and were not going to be there long enough to affect very many lives directly. But if those we encountered could catch the vision of making a difference where they lived every day, the ripple effect could be astronomical. Linda genuinely accepted the challenge to make a difference, to take a stand and to let her light shine. We prayed for Linda before we left and as a part of the prayer, thanked God for stopping her car long enough for us to get there. Then we asked Him to send someone to help her or somehow fix her car, so she could get on her way. In three or four minutes, Linda went driving by with her head hanging out of the window. She waved and yelled, "It worked. It started right up. God healed my car!"

The timing of meeting Linda was quite amazing. When we considered all the many stops we made that day, the people we had spoken to for an exact amount of time, the lunch break we took, and the phone calls we received, all of which put us at the exact location where Linda was sitting at the exact time she was sitting there, we could not help but be amazed by God's split-second timing. True, we had prayed for those kinds of divine appointments for months before the walk started, but when we saw them materialize before our very eyes, we couldn't help but be in awe.

The timing during the walk across America was always a delicate balance between stepping and stopping. We had to walk at the right speed, in the right direction, and on the right path. We had to start and end at the right places and genuinely be sensitive to God. And the most wonderful part? This balance wasn't achieved tediously or with an overriding fear we might misstep. It became as natural as…well…as natural as walking. We sensed the nudges in one direction or the other, saw open doors and opportunities, and knew He was directing our paths. Even though there was still much pain, discomfort, and fatigue, walking became the joy of our lives, because walking meant finding people and sharing the message, He had given us to share. The message was one of hope, love, restoration, and reconciliation. A message we loved to share. And…so we walked.

Chapter 18

The next two weeks would illustrate how drastically different two seven-day periods of time could be. Our attitude, our driver's spiritual awareness and support, and the intensity of the spiritual warfare being waged against us, all impacted the effectiveness of our journey.

Our weeks were spent with volunteer drivers. These people, many of whom we barely knew, would be living with us for the week. We came to find out that regardless of how wonderful someone was, adding another person to already cramped living quarters, especially after the kind of grueling, physically demanding days we were experiencing, could stretch hospitality and Christian love to the limits.

When our driver for week nine arrived, he shocked us by announcing he had prayed for an "uneventful" week. At first, this seemed a little odd. We assumed anyone walking across America was expecting every week to be eventful. I wasn't sure what Cliff meant, but by the end of the walk, I was amazed at the spiritual insight which had led him to pray as he had.

Cliff's week with us was wonderful. He was among a select group of drivers who did everything right. He was always where he was supposed to be when he was supposed to be there. He scouted out old, abandoned sections of Route 66 for us enabling us to get off the Interstate. He ran errands at night to get what we needed. He worked on inventing new pads for Jane's feet to cushion her blisters. He used the less-than-perfect facilities at our primitive campground to give us a little more privacy. He was supportive, encouraging and above all else, didn't show up with a hundred ideas on how to do what we were doing, "better". Even after returning home, Cliff sent us a care package with lots of needed items including dog repellent, which probably saved us from severe injury later in the walk.

Cliff understood something many of our drivers did not: The continuation and ultimate completion of The Walk to Reclaim America had to be the most important thing of the week. We asked those who came to help for a week to make the same commitment we had made for six months; to do whatever was necessary to make sure our goal of walking across the United States was accomplished. Cliff had prayed for a week free of distractions which could have derailed that goal. It turned out to be a brilliant prayer.

Not only was his prayer insightful, but it was also powerfully answered. Even though during that week we walked at over 7000 feet elevation, nearly 100 miles on the Interstate, in a blinding snowstorm, in rain, in heat and in cold, we had no major setbacks. God knew this week would be one of stepping and not so much stopping. That's one reason why Cliff's attitude and answered prayers were so precious.

We did have a few encounters though, like Anthony, a carpet layer from the area. He stopped and asked us for directions. I can't remember how many times local residents asked us for directions, but it always made us chuckle as they drove away. As we shared the gospel with Anthony, he told us he had a Christian wife who was fasting and praying for his salvation. Hopefully, our encounter with Anthony was one more step in the process of him coming to Christ. Then down the road, we met an African American couple who were team-driving a truck across the country. They were from Mississippi and the woman was a believer. We had a chance to share with the man and encourage him to come to know Christ.

As we were nearing the east edge of Moriarty, New Mexico, Jane had an encounter while I was talking on the phone. John was working at a tire store and had been raised in the Salvation Army. Jane's smiling face and captivating personality caused people, but especially men, to open up to her almost immediately. John shared that his wife had left him. He was alone and hurting. Our path had led us to the place where he was working at just the right time. Jane had prayer with him in the parking lot of the tire store.

Moriarty was the only town we walked through that week but even on the Interstate and in places along the highway God brought people across our path. A couple from Texas pulled over onto the shoulder to check on us. A woman named Rose in the restroom with Jane who had had a "bad year" asked for prayer. A truck driver who happened to be from Jane's hometown of Oklahoma City was broken down on the highway. He was a captive audience as we shared about the walk. A car from Crossville, TN, one of our favorite places to minister, pulled into the parking lot where we were eating lunch. We used our connection to Crossville as an icebreaker and were able to share the gospel with the driver and her parents. Over and over, we saw God order our steps in a way that we would never have been able to do by planning or manipulation.

Cliff's week went in the books as one of the smoothest of the walk. In addition to keeping on schedule, having numerous encounters with hurting people, and making lots of great memories, Cliff even managed to talk a local auto parts store into donating enough motor oil and filters to maintain the camper and support van for the rest of the walk. What a testimony this week was of how wonderful things could be when our driver came prayed up, focused and willing to give up personal desires and agendas to become an integral part of the Walk.

The contrast would come almost immediately. We did not have a driver for the next week scheduled, prompting us to make an urgent plea. Finally, someone volunteered but arrived a day late. She had self-doubt. She had family issues at home. She was not used to being away from her husband. Her cell phone wouldn't work. She had issues with directions, especially driving directions, and simply couldn't follow instructions. I believe she came out of a sincere desire to help, but somehow that all got tangled up in lots of personal issues. Her focus was inward. As a result, the week turned into a chain of one disastrous event after another. "Lost" probably sums up the week as well as any word could. Our driver was lost from us, we were lost from her, time was lost, opportunities were lost, our enthusiasm for the walk was temporarily lost, and most unfortunate of all, in one circumstance, our testimony was probably lost. Jane and I both battled anger (not always successfully), and discouragement and because our driver came late and left early, we also faced walking without a driver for two days, an almost impossible task, especially in the desert.

The contrast between the two weeks was remarkable. One week everything seemed to go right and the very next week everything seemed to go wrong. We learned a very deep spiritual lesson because of these two weeks. Our eyes were opened to how vulnerable we all are when we 1) let our guard down, 2) lose our focus, and 3) are not in spiritual harmony with others. It was a difficult and costly lesson to learn one-third of the way through the walk, but the lesson served us well. Although we would face even greater battles ahead, physically and spiritually, we would never again let anything derail us from the task God had given us.

There were two meaningful experiences that came out of this experience. The first didn't seem positive when we were going through it, but it proved to be a morale booster later in the walk. On the first and last day of this week, we had no driver. This meant we had to find a way to walk without the periodic arrival of the van with fresh water, shoes, socks, and food. On the first day, we had the owner of the campground take us out about 14 miles west of the campground and drop us in the desert. We had packed a backpack with food, water, medicine, powder, socks, shoes, and other supplies for the day. We climbed through a barbed wire fence behind an old, abandoned Stuckey's which had most recently served as an adult bookstore. This hike was the most primitive thus far. There were no restrooms, no stores, no people and of course, no drivers within walkie-talkie range. We walked on the back side of the desert, and followed railroad tracks, with no roads or people in sight for most of those 14 miles. I was also carrying a fully loaded backpack which was something I would only have to do a few times during the walk, thank God!

As physically difficult as this trek was, it was among the most beautiful of the entire walk. The desert was just beginning to emerge from winter hibernation. The day was sunny and hot and was eerily silent except for the sound of our steps. The aroma of the dessert blooms combined with the colors of New Mexico's landscape made the morning walk a sensory pleasure. It was one of those experiences which was so spiritually invigorating, so surreal, that even now, it's hard to believe it happened.

We walked 14 miles back to the campground, had lunch, and then had the owner of the campground take us out 8 miles east of the campground where he dropped us off once again. That afternoon we walked back to camp, this time from the other direction, completing 22 miles without a driver. We later looked back at this day and drew strength from the fact we were able to accomplish so much with God's help.

The second memorable event of the week happened on Friday evening. Part of our routine each week was to find a good Mexican restaurant wherever we were and treat ourselves to a good meal. We also liked to take our driver as a way of saying thanks. Not surprisingly, this week turned out to be a bit different. Our driver refused our invitation, but Jane and I really needed a break after this incredibly stressful week, so we decided to go alone. It was a difficult meal to get through because what was normally a victory celebration ended up being a pity party. As we sat there, however, we noticed a Hispanic family sitting at the next table. One of the family members at the table was a very young mother with her infant son. We watched them play with the baby and to be quite honest, the sound of the baby laughing and the family having so much fun temporarily took our minds off our own troubles. We noticed during our meal that the little boy had a very severe cleft palate. I was moved with compassion and sensed in my spirit I needed to pray for him. I shared with Jane that I felt impressed to pray but didn't want the family to be uncomfortable. As the family was getting up to leave, I found a gentle way to ask the baby's name and I put my hand on his little body. As Jane continued the conversation, I silently prayed for Patrick. After the family was gone my eyes welled up with tears. I cried partly for Patrick and his family and the hardship and pain his physical appearance might cause them in the future. But mostly I cried for me and the fact I had allowed things so much less important to steal my joy and focus during the week which was ending.

On Saturday we moved camp to Amarillo, Texas. After arriving, we again packed our backpacks and hired a taxi to take us out of town 13 miles and drop us. Usually, we walked our miles on Saturday morning, then broke camp and moved. On this day, however, we had been up since 4 am, packed, hooked up the support van, driven 115 miles, set up camp in Amarillo, and eaten lunch. We were exhausted before we even started. These miles were out of sequence, but since we were operating without a driver and didn't want to get behind, we decided to walk where we were and where we had the ability to hire a taxi.

It was a totally urban hike; city streets, inner-city neighborhoods, Interstate crossroads, business districts, and one of the largest railroad yards in the country. As we walked through Amarillo Saturday afternoon we came upon a giant mass of railroad tracks, switching mechanisms, and trains. The railroad yard was so big, it had its own tower to control the traffic, just like an airport. Our first thought was to weave our way through the trains, over the tracks and to the other side. But as we started to walk through the yard some of the trains started to move without warning. They were going in both directions, starting and stopping, and it was just too dangerous to dodge our way through. There was a railroad office nearby, so we decided to go in and see how we might be able to get through to the other side. As we started into the office two men came out. They were engineers who had just gotten done with their run for the week. We shared with them what we were doing and asked if there was any way through the tracks. Of course, they said, "No". They did offer to drive us to the other side of the tracks on their way to the motel. We reluctantly agreed. We kept track of where they drove us and came back the next week to make up that part of the walk another way, so as not to miss those steps. This obstacle gave us a chance to talk with two more folks about Jesus with whom we otherwise would never have had the chance to talk.

Those 13 miles seemed like at least 20. Hot and exhausted, we had almost reached the truck stop where the taxi had picked us up when we met John. John was a trucker, out for a walk, maybe for exercise or maybe to get away from the cab of his truck for a while. We started one last conversation for the day, eventually getting to the question that was always on our minds, "Do you know Jesus?"

Without missing a beat, John responded, "Well, I've actually got a few problems with Jesus." As we talked a little more, John shared that he wasn't nearly as upset with Jesus as he was with some of His people. We tried to leave John with at least two fewer reasons to have a problem with Jesus, or at least with His people. The longer we walked the more we realized that walking was just a way of trying to show people who Jesus is and what He's really like. People need to know that. And…so we walked.

Chapter 19

Parts of the walk were unquestionably about changing us as we walked. We had been transformed in so many wonderful ways during the first third of the walk. God had taught us so much about Himself and His sufficiency. He had shown us so much about ourselves and our love for one another. He also reminded us time and again how important the prayers of our friends and family at home were to our safety and continued provision. The churches in our hometown met monthly to pray for us and lift us up. The prayer team at our home church continued to call throughout the entire trip to encourage us when times were tough.

There were also times when the walk was about those we met along the way. Only time will tell the significance of what we shared with those we met. There is no doubt in my mind we will spend eternity with many whom we pointed toward the Savior along the route from Santa Monica Pier to Washington D.C.

God chose to use the walk across America to affect change in other Christians as well. Sometimes it was the volunteer drivers who came to spend a week with us. That's what happened the next week as we walked across the Texas panhandle. We had walked out of sequence the preceding Saturday when we moved camp from Tucumcari, New Mexico to Amarillo, Texas and had no driver. So, when Jackie came to drive the next week, we had to go back to the New Mexico/Texas state line to begin our week. Jackie was a friend from our church back home. She was a huge NASCAR fan. The first day Jackie drove for us we were walking on I-40 near the Texas border. We noticed a caravan of semis pulling brightly colored trailers with NASCAR logos on the side. Suddenly, our walkie-talkie came to life with Jackie screaming on the other end. "Did you see that?" Jackie yelled. "Those were all the NASCAR 'haulers' that carry the cars from race to race." Jane and I couldn't have cared much less, but it was obvious Jackie was excited. When she caught up to us within a few miles, she was still beside herself. She couldn't believe God had given her that special blessing and confirmed her willingness to come to drive for us on short notice. Her spiritual experiences were only beginning.

Jackie observed us as we shared all week. She saw God move in miraculous ways each day. That week we witnessed God's protective hand as we walked through construction areas with huge earthmovers carrying tons of dirt and gravel just a few feet away from us. She saw Jane carried each day by the power of God even though her feet were covered in blisters and her big toe now had no toenail. By the end of her time with us she shared with Jane that her spiritual life had become lukewarm and being a part of such a grand adventure had challenged her in her walk with God. Along the way that week, she started sharing her faith with others. By the time Jackie left to return home she had made her own personal decision to witness and share the glorious gospel with others more consistently. We kept in touch with Jackie after the walk and watched her accept a call into a unique ministry. She got the training she needed to become a racetrack chaplain. She became the only spiritual connection many of the drivers had to God. Later Jackie was called to pastor the United Methodist Church in her hometown. We feel honored to have played a small part in Jackie's spiritual journey and she has become a lifelong friend.

We didn't indulge in many tourist attractions on the walk across America. There was little time for such indulgences and even less money. However, when we realized our walk would take us through Groom, Texas, the site of the largest cross in the Western Hemisphere, we knew it deserved a little extra time.

The morning we were to walk past the cross was cold and rainy. In addition, there were wildfires burning across the Texas panhandle and at times the smoke blowing across the road made it impossible to see more than a few feet. In short, it was anything but a perfect day to see such a glorious sight. Earlier in her quiet time, Jane had read about the story behind the hymn, *Trust and Obey*. The lyrics spoke to Jane's heart that morning and so as we walked in the cloudy, smoky, rainy weather, she began to sing:

"When we walk with the Lord,

In the light of His way,

What a glory He sheds on our way!"

As she sang the words over and over, the rain stopped, the smoke cleared, and the sun began to shine down on the road directly in front of us. He was shedding His glory on our way. Once again, God had affirmed our steps, as we took them as if to say, "When *your* way is *My* way, there is always going to be glory."

As it turned out, God had also ordered our steps so the huge cross, which can be seen for miles in all directions (on a clear day), was at exactly the 1200-mile mark of our walk. We ended the day where we had begun the journey so many steps before, basking in His presence and glory, at the foot of the cross. For those of us who love Jesus and are eternally grateful for His sacrifice, life's most meaningful moments most always begin or end at the foot of the cross. It is here we find mercy, strength and guidance. And it is here, where we invite others to kneel and find the same.

An interesting thing happened in Groom, Texas after our visit to the cross. We stopped at a convenience store for a restroom break and met a young man coming out of the store who inquired about our walk. (Jane and I usually dressed alike and carried packs which made it obvious we weren't just out for a stroll). We shared with him what we were doing and then asked him about his relationship with Christ. He immediately became angry. He cursed, got into his car, slammed the door and squealed his tires as he took off down the highway. Both of us looked at each other in disbelief. How could anyone who lived in the shadow of the cross, the largest in our part of the world, be so antagonistic about the gospel of Jesus Christ?

It made me consider the fact that many live in the shadow of crosses, church steeples, billboards or bumper stickers about Jesus. Millions live within earshot of pastors, evangelists and radio preachers. Some have become numb to the tragedy and triumph of the cross. Others have had its truth nullified by the inconsistent lifestyles of those who identify themselves as having been affected by the power of the cross. One truth was proven again and again as we encountered people across America: While the cross is loved and adored by those who see it as the power of God for salvation, it is hated by those who are offended by its convicting presence and seen as foolish by those who cannot embrace the simplicity of its message. The cross is a sword that divides those who accept it from those who reject it.

This brings me to an interesting and unexpected emotional issue Jane and I dealt with along the way. If the cross is a sword, then those who bear its message become soldiers whose duty it is to allow the cross to do its work of separating those who accept from those who reject it. It is not our job to judge or make the determination of who stands on which side of the cross. However, carrying the message of the cross makes it plain that some have made or are in the process of making what could be a final, eternity-determining choice. There were times when Jane and I walked away from a person who by their own testimony had rejected the message of God's love repeatedly. We wondered if we were being used by God to give a person one last opportunity to say yes. That could prompt some to hesitate in sharing the gospel, but it became a driving force for us. We never knew when the next person would say yes to the love of Christ and pass from one side of the cross to the other.

The few days spent walking through the Texas panhandle were rainy and cold. Once again, we found our rain gear really wasn't waterproof, especially when walking 20-plus miles each day. In addition, wildfires which had spread over much of the area made breathing difficult. On Saturday we had to quit walking early because of the low visibility caused by the smoke. We experienced every possible kind of weather on the walk. Sometimes it was merely an inconvenience, but other times, as we would eventually find out, it was downright dangerous.

As we neared the Oklahoma border Jane got more and more excited. Oklahoma is her home state and where her family lives. Being in Oklahoma City would give us a chance to see Jane's family and Rebekah, our middle child. We would also reach the halfway point of the walk, Oklahoma's state capitol building. The morning we walked into Oklahoma was the only day there was measurable snow on the ground. It snowed a blizzard in Clines Corner, New Mexico but it never stuck to the ground. It snowed in the desert outside Gallup, New Mexico but simply turned the clay to mud. This unexpected cold snap brought snow, sleet and slick roads but fortunately, it would be the last time we would see snow on the walk.

Many pastors were less than sympathetic to the walk across America. Some would not talk to us at all. We were blessed when there were those like Pastor Kendall in Elk City, Oklahoma. He instantly embraced the message of the walk and opened the doors of his church for us to speak on the Sunday we spent in Elk City. On Monday morning, Pastor Kendall decided to walk with us for the first few hours to get a little taste of what the walk was like. The temperature was just above freezing, and it drizzled frozen rain all morning. Pastor Kendall walked eight and a half miles with us. As we walked, we shared with him about divine appointments and he got to see evidence of them in his own city. Time after time we walked into situations at just the right time to share the story of Jesus. God used the walk to remind good men of God like Pastor Kendall about His perfect timing. A few days after we left Elk City, Pastor Kendall called my cell phone with the exciting news. He had been prompted early that morning to go to a convenience store and wait. This was totally out of his comfort zone and he resisted at first. Finally, he went to the store and sat down. No sooner had he arrived than a man walked in whom he had been trying to get an appointment with for months. The man sat down and joined the pastor for coffee. At last, he was able to share the Good News with him.

The week we spent camping in Elk City was also the week when we hosted our oldest volunteer driver of the walk. Sally was nearly eighty years old. She drove from Oklahoma City to join us for the week. When she arrived, her car was loaded with food, snacks and camping supplies, including a small tent. Sally intended to spend the week camping outside and cook her own food on the campfire. She had been showered with the provisions by her home church, Dumas Avenue Baptist Church. The weather was so cold and wintry that we simply could not let Sally stay outside. She slept on the sofa bed in our camper and ate with us. She did a wonderful job all week of following directions and being where she needed to be. It may not sound like much, but when you've walked all day and it's time to be done, you really want the driver to be where they are supposed to be. Well, Sally did everything right. She made notes and double-checked the directions, so she didn't get lost. It all worked well...until Friday afternoon. We made our last bathroom stop of the day and were heading out for the last three or four miles. We told Sally to go one mile down the road and wait for us. We knew there was a tricky turn at that intersection and we wanted to be able to show her what to do. Somehow, she didn't hear us. She drove off and when we arrived at the one-mile mark 20 minutes later, there was no Sally. We waited, tried to contact her on the walkie-talkies, and called her cell phone, but no Sally. We decided to keep walking. We walked for another hour to our destination for the day. Every few minutes we tried to contact Sally. Nothing. We had no vehicle; we were miles from the campground and had walked well over one hundred miles that week. We were exhausted. While we waited, some folks from Pastor Kendall's church came by. Then the pastor's wife arrived. Soon we had the sheriff and several people from the church looking for Sally. Nothing. Finally, Pastor Kendall called and told us they had located her eleven miles down the road, just sitting there waiting on us. We never were sure how Sally got so confused and we never did tell her exactly how far off course she was. We all went out for Mexican and tried to forget about the fiasco.

    We sure got an education from people like Sally. Most of our drivers were people who sacrificed to come. They didn't have a lot of money. Most took their vacation time to drive for us. Some did better than others. Some were harder to live with, but they all had servants' hearts and we could not have completed the walk without their help. Their contribution was more than driving a support vehicle. They prayed for us as we walked. They encouraged us when we were hurting. They ran errands in the evening and one driver even waved flags and cheered for us every time we approached the van (to be honest, that got a little old after a few days). It reminded us once again about how everyone in the family of God has a place and a purpose.

God didn't ask them to walk across America...that was our calling. He did prompt them to come alongside us and help in an invaluable way. Working together we were able to accomplish what we could not have accomplished alone.

Another lesson was driven home about this time while walking with Pastor Kendall that cold, rainy morning. We stopped by a gas station and as people were filling up their cars, we struck up conversations with them about the walk hoping it would lead to a discussion about spiritual things. A white pick-up truck (the vehicle of choice in Oklahoma) drove in and two men got out. They were assigned to work together each day. One of the men was an associate pastor of a local African American congregation. The other man, Preston, was not a follower of Christ. We saw this phenomenon over and over across America: One believer and one non-believer paired together for eight hours each day. It was amazing how many times it had never occurred to the believer the importance of sharing their faith with the other person. There they were, with a captive audience inside a pick-up truck or sitting across from each other at the office, yet their Sunday faith was never allowed to filter into their Monday through Friday routine. Sometimes the non-believer was even surprised to hear their fellow worker was a Christian.

Relationships are never an accident. Jane and I saw how friendships formed over many years made the walk possible for us. Those we had come to know in the years leading up to the walk became some of our biggest supporters. But relationships with non-believers are not an accident of chance either. God has a way of pairing us up with people who need our encouragement, our spiritual guidance, our advice and our witness. One of our greatest blessings was walking away from a situation like this with a fellow Christ-follower recommitted to sharing his or her faith with those with whom they worked.

Practically every day God reminded us we were a part of His plan in someone else's life. The walk wasn't only about what we were doing, but it was also about God using us in other people's lives. It was easy to get self-absorbed in our own pain, our own accomplishments and our own agenda. God kept us humble by showing us time and again we were merely His servants, doing His bidding and fulfilling a very small role in His big design. We wanted to be a part of that plan, and…so we walked.

Chapter 20

Walking across America was without a doubt the most intense learning experience of our lives. It seemed every day brought new lessons about human nature, God's creation and our own weaknesses. Life lessons emerged from a variety of sources, but sometimes it was the road itself that taught us.

Old Route 66 varies in its condition from near Interstate quality to what's left of disintegrating asphalt to dirt paths where the roadbed once existed. Some of it has been abandoned, allowing time and weather to take their toll, never to be resurrected again. Other parts of the old route are maintained because it is still a useful means of transportation, connecting one small town to another. Such is the case in Oklahoma.

Between Elk City and Oklahoma City, the old mother road is still mostly intact. The once busy road and its tourist stops are eerily quiet except for local traffic which consists of pick-up trucks pulling cattle and horse trailers and commuters trying to get to the next entrance ramp onto Interstate 40. Along this stretch of highway, one is likely to see small herds of bison, scissor-tailed flycatchers sitting on fences and lone oil pumps lazily churning the last few gallons of crude oil from tired wells. Along this stretch of highway where human encounters were few and far between God used the road to teach us about a life surrendered to Him.

Out in the country, where you can no longer hear the drone of tractor-trailers on the Interstate's asphalt, the miles pass slowly and you long for signs of civilization. But the signs you are looking for do not include an orange one that declares, "Bridge Out Ahead." A two or three-mile detour on dusty red-dirt roads in an automobile is one thing. It's a completely different matter when you're walking. As we approached the signs, we saw a crew working on what would someday be the new bridge. At this point, however, it was nothing more than a skeleton with some plywood spread across the concrete pylons. It was obvious from his demeanor that Harold, the only white man among a crew of Hispanic laborers, was in charge. His skin was dry and leathery from years in the hot Oklahoma sun. His face was frozen in a permanent scowl as he pointed and gave almost silent commands to his crew. He didn't smile and barely acknowledged us as we approached his domain. We shared with Harold about our walk and explained it would make our life easier if we could cross on the makeshift bridge. I was willing to let the opportunity for sharing about Christ pass because I didn't want to make Harold angry and lose any chance we had of avoiding a detour…but not Jane. When she asked him if he knew Jesus his response was, "Vaguely." That wasn't good enough. She politely suggested he might consider getting to know Him better. I guess Harold was impressed with her boldness. He gave her a little bit of a smile, perhaps as much as he had allowed himself to enjoy for quite some time and told us we could cross.

As we continued down the road after crossing Harold's bridge, I thought about how many times in my life I've allowed detours and difficulties to keep me from what God had for me on the other side. Sometimes it just seemed easier to take the path of least resistance and go with the flow. I wondered what I may have missed over the years because I was intimidated by the dangers ahead or the gruff naysayers in my path. What we experienced was a lesson learned scores of times on our walk… "God will make a way where there seems to be no way."

Not long after we crossed Harold's little bridge, we approached the longest bridge on the entire length of Route 66. The bridge is 3,944 feet long; nearly 4/5ths of a mile. If you were traversing this bridge in an automobile, you wouldn't give it a second thought. However, this bridge had no shoulder, and for walkers, that signals trouble. If two cars were crossing in opposite directions at the same time, something or someone had to go, and it was probably not going to be one of the cars. In retrospect it seems humorous, but we did look over the bridge to see where we might jump in an emergency. The South Canadian River is extremely shallow here and jumping would not have been a good option. We stood on one side of the bridge counting cars and timing how long it took them to cross. Although this wasn't a busy bridge, we knew in the fifteen minutes it would take to cross it, there would likely be some traffic. We thought about calling our driver and having him drive us across, but we hated to interrupt the unbroken chain of steps from the West Coast to now. Convinced we could make it, we started to walk. During the trek across the bridge, only a few cars crossed and never two at the same time. God had again ordered our steps in perfect harmony with circumstances.

The long bridge taught us another important lesson: Calculating and figuring can only get you to a certain point. At some point, you must step out and trust He is in control and has ordered things, so you will be able to accomplish what He has called you to do. We saw this proven over and over on our journey. For example, in the months preceding the walk, we spent a disproportionate amount of time on the budget. We had slashed expenses down to ridiculous levels, yet when we took our first steps away from Santa Monica Pier, we were less than fifty percent funded. We knew there was at least a chance, humanly speaking, we'd get halfway and need to suspend the walk. We had determined if we had to spend a few months along the way working secular jobs to raise the funds necessary to complete the walk, we were willing. But God provided over and over. During the walk, God continued to use unexpected sources to meet our needs. People filled up our vehicles with gas, bought our meals, and paid our camping fees. Planning was beneficial. It was necessary. Planning, however, is never intended to limit what we dream or what we accomplish. It's meant to measure the greatness of our God when He provides. Consider the five thousand Jesus fed. The disciples devised a budget to feed them. Jesus didn't criticize the calculations. Philip's number crunching serves as an eternal reminder of the greatness of Jesus' power to surpass what human resources could accomplish. Our reasoning, that warm Spring day in Oklahoma said, "There's no way to make it across that bridge without a problem." God said, "Just do what I've asked you to do, and I'll take care of everything else." One of the unique things about Route 66 is the way it was constructed. Much of it was poured in sections, twelve feet long or so, then joined together with expansion joints. I still remember driving to California with my family in 1966 on Route 66 and hearing the monotonous "thump, thump, thump" every few seconds as our brand-new Pontiac Catalina sped along the highway. There are parts of the old road where you can still see those original sections. Often though, the old sections of Portland cement have been covered over with asphalt. If you look closely, you can see where the original expansion joints have popped up, causing a bump in the road's surface. We noticed this on several occasions and marveled that no matter how many layers of asphalt had been laid over the top of the old sections, the bumps still resurfaced. One afternoon it occurred to me those bumps were an awful lot like sin in our lives. Our tendency is to cover over sin, especially the recurring kind which seems to annoy us with its aggravating "thump, thump, thump" presence in our lives. We don't want the sin, but we don't want to deal with the root problem either. Somewhere in the bedrock of our lives, there are faulty assumptions, detrimental habits, or foundational untruths about God with which we need to deal. This requires a commitment few are willing to make. Instead, we cover up the bumps with another layer of religiosity. It doesn't work. It never has, and it never will.

Some lessons the road taught us came easy; some were painful to learn. One of the recurring lessons was: Your destination is determined by the path you take. Every evening we continued to pour over maps and check computer programs for the road which would lead us to the next destination. We learned early and often, you will end up where the road takes you, not necessarily where you hope it takes you. Roads are funny that way. Tragically, many still believe they can walk the wrong road yet end up in the right place.

We were determined to end up in Washington D.C. on the steps of the Supreme Court. That's where we believed God had called us to finish our walk. So, we picked the paths that would lead us there, without regard to the hardships faced along those roads. We knew if we kept putting one foot in front of the other long enough, as long as we were on the right path, we would end up where we intended. And…so we walked.

Chapter 21

For longer than we could remember, Oklahoma City had been a greatly anticipated milestone. Oklahoma City was where we would leave Route 66 for other routes which would lead us more directly to our destination. This was Jane's hometown. We would be greeted by family and friends for the first time in over 1400 miles. Most importantly, Oklahoma City, we had calculated, was exactly halfway. Until this point, there had always been more than half of the journey ahead. That led to some doubt as to whether our bodies, and especially Jane's feet, could tolerate the continual punishment of walking twenty miles or more, six days per week. Somehow, knowing we had conquered the first half signaled fresh hope we might finish the journey we had started three months earlier.

Oklahoma City also allowed us to have contact with hundreds of people each day. The road from Amarillo to OKC had been mostly deserted. The weather had been cool, rainy and foggy, which discouraged people from being outside as we walked through small towns. Springtime thunderstorms with accompanying tornado warnings kept people inside as well. We had been close enough to see a twister in western Oklahoma. But that was behind us for now.

On the last few days of March 2006, the weather was warm, and the skies were blue. People were out on the streets in short sleeves, and we walked with a new determination to get to the halfway point and beyond. We could not walk for more than a few yards at a time without talking to someone. There was Ronnie, an African American man who had found Christ in prison. Karen, a Seminole Native-American, Fredrico and Hosea, both Hispanic, and Vickie whose car was not running, so she was waiting for a bus to take her to work. Earl Leroy Taylor was a homeless man in downtown OKC who wore a funny-looking bright green hat. Jane had three dollars in her pocket, given to her a couple days earlier by a cigar-smoking, pick-up-driving man in overalls. She gave those three dollars to Earl Leroy for breakfast.

As we walked another block or two, we could begin to see the memorial built on the site of the Oklahoma City bombing. Jane and I had already prayed thousands of prayers as we had walked across half of America. We cried many times as we prayed over schools, with hurting people and for spiritual healing in our land. But something unexplainable happened that morning as we saw those 168 chairs, representing those who had died on April 19, 1995. We could not hold back the tears as we realized this memorial symbolized in an inexplicable way the uncertainty of life, the unpredictability of death and the importance of our mission to share the love of God with everyone we met. It exemplified the spiritual battle which goes on every day in our world and that we have an enemy whose purpose it is to steal, kill and destroy. But it also reminded us we serve a God who loved us so much He sent His Son, so we might have life.

As we stood there looking at the memorial, praying for the survivors and families of those who were killed, we forgot for a few moments about our own pain and discomfort. We thanked God our family had never had to endure such heartache and asked that He continue to safely lead us to our destination.

As we stood in front of the memorial, we noticed a news reporter and cameraman walking toward us. Channel 9 in Oklahoma City was there to cover the walk across America. Over the course of the first three months, we were interviewed by numerous radio stations, newspapers and television stations. People from one end of the county to the other were praying for us after hearing our story. Some of our drivers came because of hearing about us on the radio, even though they had never met us in person until they arrived. God used the media in wonderful ways during the walk. We were talked about on blogs, many of which were not Christian in nature. For example, one of the websites about Route 66 kept their readers updated as to our progress all the way to Washington D.C. The coverage was not always positive, but it was generally accurate, and we had an opportunity with each interview to share the gospel of Jesus Christ. We were even covered by a reporter from National Public Radio.

When our interview was over with the television station, we received a call from "The Oklahoman," Oklahoma City's major newspaper. The reporter wanted to meet us for a sit-down interview. We agreed, and that newspaper article turned out to be one of the best of the entire walk (except for the final one)! Winding our way through downtown continued to give us multiple opportunities to share Jesus with those we encountered. Even though we were walking through the city which has been referred to as the "buckle on the Bible belt," many people we talked to admitted not having a personal relationship with Jesus. We learned there are no places so saturated with the gospel where the light of the Good News is not needed.

One of the unexpected pleasures of our time in Oklahoma City came in the form of State Representative Mike Reynolds. He is a wonderful Christian politician who heard about our walk across America and wanted to do something special for us to commemorate the halfway point. Representative Reynolds drew up a resolution endorsing the Walk to Reclaim America and invited us to attend the session where the resolution would be read and adopted by the Oklahoma House of Representatives. It was an unbelievable honor. The resolution was adopted unanimously by the Representatives and then we were taken to the State Senate and introduced there. We were given a standing ovation both times. This would have been an unbelievable honor anywhere, but the fact it happened in Jane's home state made it especially wonderful.

The next day we walked to the State Capitol building to officially mark the halfway point. There we were met by our daughter Rebekah, many friends from churches in the OKC area where we had ministered, and then, just as we were getting ready to leave the Capitol building who should pull up in a cab but Pastor Mark from our home church. He presented us with the wonderful gift of a two-night stay in a luxury hotel from our friends back home. He also came and walked with us through Oklahoma City that afternoon, and it's a good thing he did. There were so many people there were times when Pastor Mark, Jane and I were all talking to different people at the same time. It was simply amazing.

As we walked with Pastor Mark, we saw a young boy on the sidewalk jumping rope. It seemed odd a young boy wouldn't be in school and that he'd be alone on the street. As we walked past him, I was drawn to look back and there, in the large van, was a mom and a little girl. It was one of those times when I couldn't keep walking, I had to go back. I introduced our group of three to the mom and told her about the walk. While I was talking, I noticed they were fixing peanut butter and jelly sandwiches in the van for lunch. It all seemed very unusual and we knew something wasn't right. After sharing with her about the walk and finding out she was a believer, she said, "You know, we've had just a terrible morning. It seemed like our world was coming to an end. But now after hearing about your walk, it just kind of puts everything into perspective." We had prayer with her and walked on. A little while later their van pulled up beside us and the kids jumped out. They gave us cold water and oranges. We always refer to them as the PB&J kids. What a blessing Thomas and Sophie Grace were to us.

Our brief pause in the middle of the country was about to be over, but there was to be one more celebration. We had planned from the beginning to have a halfway rally in OKC. We encouraged friends and families from various periods in our ministry to come and help us kick off the second half of the walk. It was simply amazing. Southern Hills Baptist Church opened its doors to us for the rally. There were people from the first two churches I served as youth pastor back in my college days. There were many people from churches in Oklahoma City, Cushing, Tuttle, Crescent, El Reno and Edmond Oklahoma. There were even people from Tennessee and Arkansas and of course, Pastor Mark from Ohio. The entry in Jane's journal from the next day said it all: "It was like all of our worlds, past and present...all collided in a really good way!"

God used scores of people to encourage us and bless us along the way. The halfway point was no exception. The night of the rally, the members of a very small church in OKC, Dumas Avenue Baptist Church, boarded their church bus and came to the rally. They filled the first three pews in the huge auditorium. They had, by far, the largest single group present. This is a struggling church in an economically depressed area of OKC. Jane and I had gone there to minister for several years in a row. That night, they not only brought the largest group of people but gave the most sacrificially. When we opened the envelope they gave us, we found over $500 in cash and gift cards for use on the trip. We were humbled time and again as God met our needs, not through the wealthy, but through His humble servants who simply said "yes" when He called.

There were times when it wasn't about financial support but about moral and physical support. The day after the rally in Oklahoma City, Pastors Doug Melton and Jeff Leduc from Southern Hills Baptist came and walked with us. These men pastor a very large church with many responsibilities and demands on their time. Taking time to walk and talk with us was an incredible encouragement. Their presence was their way of saying "yes" to God.

When God first began to speak to Jane and me about walking across America, something occurred to us. We were probably not the first people He had asked to walk across our country, pray for and share His love with its people and do it completely by faith. We were not the most qualified or the most capable. We were not the most athletic or the best funded. If He started asking from the top of the "most likely to succeed" list, we had to have been near the bottom. Our greatest qualification for this task came, not from our ability, but our willingness. That's all God is interested in…the ones who will say "yes." We did…and so we walked.

Chapter 22

Something changed about the walk after the halfway point. Even after several years of analyzing it, I'm still not sure what happened, but something changed. By this point, we had walked over 1400 miles. Jane had walked in pain almost every day. Her blisters came and went but there was not a single day after the first week when at least some part of her feet were not blistered. We were now facing the most brutal temperatures of the walk. Most of the remaining days would be spent walking with the heat index near or above 100 degrees. We had literally dragged ourselves into Oklahoma City on pure adrenaline, anticipating the halfway point. We asked ourselves, "How could we do this for three more months?"

Emotionally we were drained. Every week was like starting all over again with our volunteer drivers. My patience was running thin with drivers who were sure they had a better system for us to try every Monday morning. We were having less and less alone time on Sunday to recover and regroup. The newspaper, television and radio coverage were now to the point where most Sundays were spent speaking at churches or being introduced to the congregation, which meant more face time with people after each service.

We had now been separated from our family (except our daughter Rebekah) and hometown friends for three months. We had a dear friend in the last stages of cancer back home. We were homesick and longed to attend a church service in our home church.

Financially we were seeing the bottom of the bank account as we paid the expenses of staying on the road. Our van, which had just rolled over to 150,000 miles, was beginning to experience major problems which produced unexpected expenses. We had emptied our house before the walk and put it on the market hoping it would sell during the early weeks of the walk. The sale of the house would have eliminated our mortgage and infused our ministry with some much-needed cash, but it was rarely shown and there were no offers.

Logistically, our routes had now become much more complicated. Up until now, we walked on Route 66, I-40, or the railroad tracks and dirt paths which paralleled both. Only a dozen times or so had we had to walk out into the desert without at least some idea of where we were headed. But now we would walk on a mishmash of roads that led east. We would stay as close to I-40 as possible, but road construction was beginning, and detours were becoming commonplace. All in all, there were dozens of reasons to quit, and some days only one real reason to carry on…obedience.

It seems unspiritual to say, but during the next couple of weeks, the walk was mostly about taking the steps and getting in the miles for the day. We were fatigued, and excitement was hard to come by. There were encounters but we were now walking in areas where many were nominal Christians who weren't excited about what we were doing. Even as we walked through the campus of our alma mater, Oklahoma Baptist University, we could generate no interest in our cross-country prayer walk. We had contacted the school, hoping that as alumni, we would be welcomed to challenge the students in their own walks of faith, but our phone calls were never returned. Although we were fairly sure no other graduates had ever done anything like this and that students could have been challenged to accept their own callings through our story, it became one more example of how those who we thought would be most supportive, simply had no interest.

There were exceptions, like Herschel, just outside of Shawnee, Oklahoma who wondered if we knew any lonely old ladies. Herschel was a believer, but lonely. Then there was Brandy, our server one night for supper. She had had ovarian cancer, but miraculously became pregnant and was anticipating a normal delivery in a month or so. We met Chad at a gas station. He was a massive African American man who, when asked about Jesus replied, "You're talkin' to a man who knows Him!" We met two women in a convenience store who had seen us on TV. They gave us free drinks and an awesome cinnamon roll. A man just returning from hunting said he'd known Jesus "for nigh onto 60 years" even though he didn't look a day over 40. Many people in Oklahoma offered to give us rides. When we told them we needed to walk every step they almost always replied, "We won't tell anyone." The pastor of First Baptist in Dustin offered us a place to stay. Our good friend Pastor Art Fox drove down from Cushing, OK one day and met us for lunch. He went into the next town and arranged for us to enjoy a huge breakfast the next morning. There were pleasant "people surprises" all along the way like Gene, a 71-year-old man picking up cans along the highway. He had invented an ingenious wooden hoop to hold his trash bags while he collected the cans. After sharing with him we walked on, but several minutes later he drove up beside us. He said, "I just wanted to pray for you." We got in a little circle beside the two-lane highway while Gene prayed. He slipped us a few dollars, probably earned when he cashed in his cans and drove off. There was no shortage of wonderful Christian people who blessed us, prayed for us, and even helped us financially. But what we longed for and missed were the people we had met in the West and Southwest who needed to hear about Jesus. They had been amazed people would walk across America to share His wonderful story. People here seemed somehow numb to the power of it all.

In retrospect, what we missed during these days was the simple joy of knowing we were doing what God had asked. He had done so many big things in the first half of the walk. Perhaps we missed some of the everyday, normal-sized blessings because we were looking too hard for the big ones. What we needed was something supernatural to jolt us back into the reality that God was a miracle-working God every single day and that's exactly what we got.

As we walked through eastern Oklahoma, the temperatures and humidity rose to the highest level of the walk. Even when we began walking at daybreak, by mid-morning we were drenched in perspiration and drained of energy. On Thursday morning, April 13th, we were walking just outside of Muldrow, Oklahoma. The next day would be Good Friday and as we meditated on Jesus' walk up Calvary, our steps took on a whole new meaning. Just then a car pulled up beside us and the well-dressed, sophisticated-looking woman rolled down her window. "Are you the people walking across America? I saw you on TV last night," she yelled out of the window in a very thick Oklahoma accent. Evelyn, a registered nurse, had been on her way to Tulsa to shop, but had lost interest in the trip and felt she needed to turn around. She was certain the reason was to meet us. We would soon be convinced of the very same thing. She expressed concern about us walking in the heat, and in what had become true Oklahoma fashion, offered us a ride and promised not to tell. She also admonished us to wear light colors in this heat instead of the dark blue and red that we were accustomed to wearing. She told us about a restaurant just ahead in Muldrow called *Broadway Joe's* and offered to buy lunch for us and our drivers. We agreed and continued to walk while she drove on ahead into town. By the time Jane and I arrived at the restaurant, Evelyn had already met and talked with our drivers, given them an envelope for us, and paid for our lunch. The owners of the restaurant, Marina and Joe, were also believers and the buffet they had prepared tasted just like a home-cooked meal. Evelyn said her goodbyes before lunch and promised she'd stay in touch. When we got ready to leave, Marina said Evelyn had left more than enough for the meals and after ringing us up gave Jane the change. We left a tip out of our change and Jane put the remaining money, $33 in her special place where she accumulated the money people gave us until it was needed by someone else. When we got outside, we opened Evelyn's envelope to find a $100 bill which Jane also tucked away. (Evelyn, by the way, became a life-long friend. We communicate via email and Facebook often and we exchange Christmas cards each year. We even got to stop and have lunch with her on a recent trip. After all this time, she still talks about the day she met us in that hot Oklahoma sun.)

After lunch, Dick and Bonnie, our drivers for the week, drove ahead and waited for us in a motel parking lot. When we got there, however, we could see a truck stop with a McDonald's® and we encouraged them to meet us there. This would provide bathrooms and a place for Jane to change shoes and socks in one stop instead of two. It would also allow us to replenish our supply of $5 McDonald's® gift cards which we gave out to the homeless along the way. After we used the restroom, and while Jane was sitting in the open door of the van taking care of her feet (something she did six or seven times each day), I struck up a conversation with Dan. He had a full backpack and was obviously traveling cross-country. Dan began to witness to me about Christ and when I shared what we were doing we rejoiced together. Dan was trying to get to Durango, Colorado, where he had a job waiting for him. He was a stone mason, had been out of work, and needed to be in Colorado by Monday to secure the job. Dan was afraid hitchhiking was not going to get him there on time and was wondering about buying a bus ticket, but he only had $30. Jane called the bus station and found out a bus ticket from Fort Smith, Arkansas to Durango, Colorado was $162.50. Jane counted the money which had been given to us over the last few hours and it was exactly $133. With Dan's $30 he could buy his ticket with fifty cents to spare. Although reluctant to give away every penny God had placed in our hands, we knew this was more than a coincidence. We sent Dan along with our drivers to the Greyhound® station where they purchased his ticket and put him on a bus.

God reminded us that wherever we stepped and wherever we stopped, He had gone before us setting up divine appointments. None of them were steps or stops worth millions or even thousands of dollars. No, these were steps and stops worth far greater riches than worldly gain. These were stops which had the potential of changing peoples' eternities. Dan was a former alcoholic who now ministered to the homeless and those with addictions. Getting him to the right place at the right time could have and may still be having enormous consequences for the kingdom of God. The thing is, you don't always see the consequences of your obedience. You simply know the highest sacrifice of praise is obedience…and obedience to us right now meant we must keep on walking. And…so we walked.

Chapter 23

During an experience like the Walk to Reclaim America your spiritual sensitivities are heightened. Everything seems more important, more significant. Every event seems guided by the hand of God. Late on Maundy Thursday we walked to the Oklahoma/Arkansas state line. On our way back to camp, at the end of the day, we passed a young man walking down the highway carrying a cross. This was not the first time I'd seen a man carry a cross. I had carried a cross on several occasions myself and my friend Arthur Blessitt had carried his 12-foot wooden cross around the world. But on this day before Good Friday, after walking in the blistering heat for eight hours ourselves, seeing this young man in his twenties carrying a cross down a busy highway in his sandals brought a flood of emotion. We turned around and went back to speak with him. As I stepped out of the van I began to cry before I even got to Gary. Seeing the sacrifice and dedication of this young man was such an encouragement to me. He shared that several men from his church, Roland Assembly of God, were walking up and down Highway 64 to remind people of Jesus' sacrifice. I walked back to the van encouraged that there were others who were willing to take a stand, to let their light shine and make a difference in our land.

For the next two days, we walked in Arkansas ending the week just west of Ozark. The scenery was beautiful, but the hills were long and sometimes steep. The heat had taken a toll on our physical bodies and when we settled into our campground in Russellville, Arkansas late Saturday evening, we were tempted to sleep in on Sunday morning. But it was Resurrection Sunday and we couldn't allow ourselves to miss church. Besides, Russellville Christian Center was just across the Interstate from the campground and we would be able to rest Sunday evening. The service was amazing. They introduced us during the service and afterwards the pastor gave us $100, almost completely replenishing what we had given Dan a couple days earlier.

We did get some rest that evening and were excited to return to the road Monday morning. After all, we were in Arkansas. Once we crossed this state, we'd have just Tennessee and Virginia to go. Sometime during this week, we would pass the mark where we would have less than 1,000 miles left to walk. In another week our good friend and encourager Stacy, who had helped us plan the walk, would be coming to drive for the week. It was beginning to sink in. Washington D.C. was looking more and more like a reality. It seemed all downhill from here. But the week started off badly and seemed to get worse. The heat and sun were almost unbearable on Monday. We both had cold chills and were feeling sick by the end of the day. When we got back to camp, we discovered our legs were covered in a blotchy rash. We thought about taking a day off but were barely keeping up with the schedule. We had to maintain at least 110 miles each week to reach Washington D.C. on time.

We didn't like the idea of wearing long pants the next day, but we couldn't allow our legs to get any more sun. We purchased some lightweight sweatpants and headed out into the heat. The day could have been miserable, but instead, the Lord gave us a holy distraction that kept our minds off the heat and the discomfort. Jane shared with me that as we began to walk, she felt we needed to pray for ten encounters that day. There had been only one other day with ten encounters outside a major city. People were few and far between on the two-lane back roads of Arkansas, but in faith, we started counting. First, was the lady riding her mower down the shoulder of the highway, then someone whose mower had broken down. Then, three teenagers walked down the road, and so it continued. Others crossed our path…six, seven, eight. Then Joe, a WWII vet, whom we met in a convenience store. We talked to him about his experiences and he showed us pictures and his medals which he had just shown to the history class at the local high school. We shared about the walk and its purpose and gave him two cards, at his request. When he got out his wallet to put the cards away, he pulled out two five-dollar bills and handed them to Jane. Joe was number nine and the cashier behind the counter was number ten. God had done it; the day was over. God had given us ten people to talk to in one day. Absolutely amazing.

All week, they just kept coming. Highway patrolmen who stopped to check on us heard the story of why we were walking. Truck drivers like James Bush, hauling logs, convenience store cashiers, folks fishing beside ponds and lakes and even the bag boy at Kroger all got to hear the story of our prayer walk across America. Talking about Jesus became more natural than ever in our lives. He had become so real to us. He was with us every step of the walk. It only made sense to talk about Him. Our faces glowed as we spoke of Him and how much we loved Him. Never had I been so in love with my Savior.

As we planned, the year before the walk, the weather was one factor that couldn't be predicted in advance. Walking from January through the first week in July could mean everything from below-zero temperatures with snow and ice to blistering heat and springtime storms. We had agreed to walk in every kind of weather except lightning. Getting wet wouldn't hurt us, but lightning could kill and many times as we walked in the open country, we were the tallest object (best lighting rod) around. However, we didn't know how uncomfortable walking in waterproof outerwear could be when it was nearly 100 degrees outside. On Thursday it was raining. We pulled the rubbery Gortex® over our legs, which were still covered with prickly, itching rashes. It was a combination of a whole assortment of unpleasant physical sensations. The day was horribly long, but God was faithful, as He had been every step of the way.

Friday, April 21st began as practically every other walk day had since Santa Monica, CA. The alarm sounded a little after 4 a.m. and we began the morning routine. We would spend an hour or so having our quiet time (prayer, Bible study and devotions), then eat a good breakfast. Jane would then prepare our snacks and lunch; we'd decide what clothing was appropriate for the day, pack the van and join our drivers to head out to the beginning point of the day. If all went smoothly, we'd try to begin walking by 7:30 a.m.

But first, there must be coffee. Jane and I are not typical coffee drinkers. Truth be told, we don't really like coffee…but we do need coffee. We never drank coffee until we were in our thirties. Jane came home from work one day having experienced coffee with three heaping teaspoons of Carnation® Instant Cocoa and a dollop of whipped cream. This was long before the days of Starbucks® and specialty coffee. If we had decided in the mid-1980s to market it, we would have been millionaires today. Every morning we allow ourselves the pleasure of two cups of this delicious mocha delight. This morning would be no exception…or would it?

I waited for the coffee maker to drip the last few drops into the pot and promptly poured myself a cup of the steaming, nearly boiling coffee. I carried it to the table and sat down. At this point my memory is fuzzy and I've had to rely on Jane's account to fill in the blanks. Somehow, when reaching across the table to retrieve the canister of cocoa mix, I knocked over the full cup of coffee into my lap. The pain was so intense I went into instant panic mode. According to Jane, although I have no recollection of it, I jumped up from the table, spun around and fell. I got up, ran to the shower and immediately began flushing the burnt areas with cold water. She says I was calling out to

Jesus, which I do not doubt, as I was experiencing the most intense pain of my life. At some point while standing in the shower, I began to pull myself together enough to realize my finger was hurting nearly as much as the burns. When I fell, the full weight of my body landed on my index finger which had ended up stretched over a small step in the camper, severely dislocating the middle joint. In addition, I would find out later, I had also injured a nerve in my back.

God gave me a wonderful gift when He gave me my wife. She is a rock. Crisis does not shake her, and she considers very few things to be an emergency. But on this morning Jane was a mess. She had no idea how to fix what had just happened. She tried to calm me and convince me we would figure it out, but one look at my finger told her we would have to go to the emergency room. That was a complication we did not need. We had no medical insurance and very little money. She did not know at that point how severe the burns were, but I did. I was frightened to go to the hospital and frightened not to. I avoid doctors and hospitals except in the most critical of circumstances, but with every passing moment I was convinced this situation met the criteria. The shock was wearing off and the full force of the pain emanating from all my injuries was overwhelming. I threw on some loose-fitting clothes and we climbed out of the camper and into the van. Jane drove me straight to the hospital. It was 4:30 a.m.

The activity of the next few hours quickly became a blur. The night nurse, Jonathan, took my history and statement about what had happened while Jane dealt with getting me registered at the front desk. Once on the stretcher and in the examination room, there was a constant stream of nurses, doctors and x-ray technicians coming and going. One of the most traumatic parts of the entire process was lying exposed to everyone who came and went while the burns were being evaluated. The doctor decided Jonathan should insert a catheter because of the danger of swelling from the burns. Several nurses and doctors examined my finger. They pulled and tugged and yanked but nothing happened. Jane came and went. By now she had called friends and family. She held the phone to my ear, so they could pray with me. One of the most precious calls was to my dad. I remember my father sobbing on the other end of the phone. I assured Him God was in control and even though His ways are not our ways, they are always best.

Jane was still crying. The orthopedic surgeon came in carrying my X-rays. He was not smiling. He said the injury was severe and would likely require surgery to repair it. He agreed to make a last attempt to put it back into place. They loaded the joint with more painkillers and as he firmly pulled and tugged the finger finally responded. Another x-ray confirmed the joint was temporarily aligned. He warned me I could have very limited use of the finger because of tendon and ligament damage and said I may still need surgery or at the very least, physical therapy.

While the orthopedic doctor was putting my finger in a splint, the emergency room physician, who had been on the phone, came into my room. Again, no smiles. "I think you should go to the Burn Center in Little Rock as soon as possible. You have second and third-degree burns in some very sensitive areas and you may need skin grafts. I don't feel qualified to deal with this situation here," the doctor stated very matter-of-factly. "I'll get your transfer papers ready," he said as he left the room.

The splint now held my index finger straight, with only a slight bend at the middle joint. "Your finger will have to stay in the splint for a week or two and then you will have to work it very slowly to see if the finger responds. Do you have any questions?" he asked. Even though dozens of questions swirled through my medicated and foggy brain, I responded with what had become the predominant question of the last three and half months; "Do you know Jesus?" The doctor hesitated and looked a bit confused but finally responded, "Yes." I imagine it had been a while since he confronted that question. But early that Friday morning he had to come to terms with something much more important than fingers, toes and broken bones. He had to deal with something no earthly surgeon can mend or repair. He had to consider the brokenness of the human spirit.

Yesterday I had been a relatively healthy, fifty-year-old man walking across America. I could walk twenty miles per day, day after day, and except for a few blisters and perhaps some minor sun poisoning, was not much worse for the wear. Today I was leaving the hospital in a wheelchair, catheterized with a bag strapped to my leg, my finger in a splint, my arm in a sling, and on my way to the Burn Center in Little Rock for possible skin grafts. To say I felt defeated was a gross understatement. Every person, from the nurses to the doctors said the walk was over for the foreseeable future. Recuperation from the burns would take at least two weeks and that was assuming skin grafts were not needed. Jane drove the van through a driving rain all the way to Little Rock. The trip probably took an hour, but it seemed like an eternity. The questions wouldn't stop popping into my head. What were we going to tell people back home? What about all our supporters? What if I couldn't finish the walk? How were we going to pay all these hospital bills? Would I ever have use of my finger again?

There were people praying for me literally around the world. Our youngest daughter, Shoshannah was living in China, and she was praying. We had a network of people and churches all across America already praying for the walk and now their prayers were directed toward my injuries and quick recovery. Rebekah had missionary friends all over the world from her time of service with the International Mission Board and they were now praying. All my father's pastor-friends who made up a network of prayer warriors across our country were now praying. Heaven was being bombarded with requests on my behalf and as I hobbled into the Children's Hospital Burn Center, feeling like a man who had been dragged through hell itself, I knew even Jesus Himself was interceding on my behalf.

The first call of the morning had gone to Pastor Mark's home in Harrison, Ohio shortly after we arrived at the emergency room. Pastor Mark's wife Judith told Jane he was out of town on a fishing trip with some men from the church, but she would try to get in touch with him. Later that morning Pastor Mark called Jane. He was out of town fishing alright, exactly one hour from Little Rock, Arkansas. He arrived at the Burn Center with his dad while I was still in the waiting room.

Even here, God had prearranged divine appointments. Every receptionist, nurse, aide, technician, business office representative and doctor received a personal witness about our Savior from Jane or me. Even Pastor Mark's dad was witnessing to those in the Burn Center waiting room and in the cafeteria. These places were the nooks and crannies of Arkansas where we would never have been able to share about Jesus had I not been a patient. God was honoring the prayers of His people, not only for me but by reaffirming the purpose of the walk.

God placed three wonderful Christian people in charge of my care while at the Burn Center. Nikki was my nurse. She was a devoted Catholic woman whose love for the Lord was obvious from the moment she heard my story. Dr. Hendrickson, not only a capable physician but also a professor at the school of medicine, was my very sympathetic doctor. Finally, Amanda, who had worked at a hand clinic came in to look at my finger, re-splinted it and gave me advice on how to exercise it after it came out of the splint in a couple of weeks. Several hours later, I was released from the hospital without the catheter, with no skin grafts and with instructions on how to care for the burns. I was also warned not to do any long-distance walking until I was healed.

It was late afternoon Friday when we arrived back in Russellville at the campground. We had missed an entire day of walking. Tomorrow was Saturday and also happened to be Jane's birthday. There would be no walking tomorrow, and perhaps no celebration either. Before bedtime, Rebekah arrived. She left her home in Oklahoma City as soon as she could get away. The three of us would spend the weekend together making some hard decisions about where to go from here.

Saturday, April 22nd came too quickly. I was still groggy from the pain medicine but not sedated enough to be pain-free. Every move I made hurt. The burns looked horrendous and felt even worse. I could not in my wildest dreams imagine how this could ever have a happy ending. But this was Jane's birthday and I was determined to move around some, and not completely ruin the day for her. The bright side was…at least we didn't have to walk. By afternoon I managed to get into some loose-fitting shorts and we went to *La Huertos Mexican Restaurant* to celebrate Jane's special day. It may have been the medication or the emotional nature of the day, but we all swear it was the best Mexican food we've ever eaten in our lives, and we've eaten some really good Mexican food. They donned us all with sombreros and sang to Jane. We shared with those sitting in the restaurant and with our waiters the story of the walk…the story of our Savior. I couldn't walk much, just from the van to the table, but at that table I could tell a few about Jesus. And…so we walked.

Chapter 24

The accident happened on Friday morning. By all estimates, it was going to be a couple of weeks before I could put my body through the rigors of walking long distances. Because of the location of the burns, walking was particularly painful and did not promote healing. Friday was spent in hospitals, Saturday I rested and slept most of the day except for our Mexican meal, and Sunday I rested again. We didn't try to go to church. Putting on real clothes and sitting upright for an hour was a little more than I could handle, so we watched the church where we had celebrated the halfway point, Southern Hills Baptist Church, live on the Internet.

By Monday morning, the effects of the heavy-duty painkillers administered in the hospitals had worn completely off. I didn't tolerate the oxycodone which had been prescribed very well and didn't want to take it unless I absolutely had to. My thinking was clearer now, and I had a decision to make. Should I try to walk? I knew there was no way I could walk twenty miles, but if I could walk ten or even five, we would be behind by a little less. We knew our schedule had not left room for accidents and delays. We needed to walk six days per week. On the other hand, I didn't want to hurt myself even more or get an infection which would cause an even greater delay. I needed wisdom.

I'm not sure what prompted the final decision, but I decided to walk as far as I could. I was already stir-crazy from being in the camper for three days. I needed to get back on the road. We ended Thursday afternoon on the west side of Morrilton, Arkansas. We drove out to the spot we had marked on Thursday. Because of my injuries, everything was delayed so instead of getting to Morrilton at 7:00 – 7:30 a.m. as we normally would have, we arrived at about 9:00 a.m. That fact would become very important in just a short time. As we got out of the van, Jane and I huddled to pray as we did every single morning of the walk. Usually, I prayed…but this time she prayed for me.

I could not walk at my normal pace, but I did walk. The first encounter of the day was but a few steps down the road. Bill had just been released from six months in jail. While he was in jail, he lost his home. He'd been very sick with various diseases, but he knew Jesus and praised Him openly beside the road. Then there was Amos who said he had wandered far from God, but it seemed like everyone, his friends, his mother and now even two strangers walking across America had encouraged him to come back to his Heavenly Father. His son was very sick with cancer. We had prayer with Amos in the middle of the parking lot.

As we continued up the main street in Morrilton, we spotted an old gas station/car repair shop. A young man, in his mid-to-late twenties, dressed in his dark blue mechanic's outfit was outside the shop working on a car. His shirt had his name Jeff embroidered over the left chest pocket. We greeted Jeff as we walked by and asked how his day was going. He grunted an unhappy, "Not very well." Jeff was a single dad, raising two small children. They had been asking their dad to go to church with them, but Jeff had no interest in going. As Jane and one of our drivers stood off to the side, they prayed for me and for Jeff. After sharing the beautiful story of Jesus with Jeff, I asked him if there was any reason why he couldn't accept Christ and His gift of forgiveness right then and there. Jeff looked down at the ground for what seemed like an eternity. I was determined not to let Jeff off the hook by interrupting the silence. I simply stood and waited for his response. He made marks in the dirt with his black work shoes as he continued to look downward. Finally, he lifted his head and said, "No, I can't think of any reason why I can't do that." I recounted the story once again about how God loved Jeff so much that He sent His only Son. I reminded Jeff of Jesus' death, a substitute for his own, and simply shared with him what was necessary for him to accept Christ as his personal Savior. We bowed our heads underneath the metal awning which had been constructed to give Jeff some shade as he worked on automobiles. I recited my version of a sinner's prayer and asked Jeff to put it in his own words. When we were done praying Jeff looked up with a smile on his face and a twinkle in his eyes which had not been there thirty minutes earlier. Jeff had just passed from spiritual death to spiritual life, and it showed all over.

After a few more words of encouragement, we shook hands with Jeff, gave him our card so he could keep in touch, and walked down the street. As I walked away, I realized something that gave me chills. We should have walked by Jeff's repair shop on Friday morning at 7:00 a.m. Had the accident not happened that's when we would have been there. But at 7:00 a.m. or even 7:30 a.m. Jeff's shop would not have been open, and Jeff would not have been standing outside. The accident which had delayed us not only by three days but by three days plus a couple of hours was crucial to the timing of sharing the gospel with Jeff. I honestly have no idea how all that plays out in the mind of God. I cannot even begin to figure out how God's timetable works. If we had been there at the original time, would God have sent someone else to share the gospel? I don't have the answer, but here's the great news. I don't need the answer, because God took everything and worked it together in His timing for Jeff's good and for His glory. If I am submitted to His will and my answer is always "yes," whether I feel like it or not or whether it makes sense or not, He will always work everything for good. I can't say with any certainty what would have happened had the timing worked out differently. I don't know where Jeff would have spent eternity. But this I do know; because we were there and because Jeff was there and because God's timing is always perfect, I have every assurance we will spend eternity with Jeff the mechanic from Morrilton, Arkansas in heaven. And really, that's all I need to know.

We only walked five miles, and it took me three hours, but we talked with six people, including Jeff. The next day we walked six miles. I was so sore but knew we needed to go on. As we walked through huge stacks of pine tree trunks, piled high in the lots of lumber companies, a car pulled off just ahead of us. The driver got out and started walking toward us. We thought perhaps it was someone who was going to offer us a ride or someone who had seen us on TV. As the man got closer, we realized it was Jonathan, my nurse from the emergency room. He could not believe his eyes. He knew the doctor had told me I wouldn't be able to walk for two weeks. Here we were, just four days later at the end of our second day of walking. We explained to him it was God's power and grace carrying me now as it had carried Jane hundreds of miles before. Tears welled up in his eyes as he wished us well and turned to walk back to his car. Jonathan was just one example of the hundreds of Christians who were impacted by the walk. Nominal believers saw the power of God at work through the walk in a way that challenged them to make their relationship with Him personal.

On the third day, we walked twelve miles. I would never have imagined walking that distance two days earlier. God was blessing our obedience to walk through the pain. Jane had walked with constant pain since the second week. She had never flinched at continuing to be obedient to God's call. Had she not been so faithful during all those weeks of pain, and had I not known for certain God had carried her, I probably would have been much less likely to walk through my pain. The constant irritation from walking was keeping my injuries from healing as I had hoped. I carried ointment and clean dressings in my pack and had to change them several times each day. It was inconvenient and uncomfortable, but every mile was worth it.

On Wednesday we walked into Conway, Arkansas. On the outskirts of town, we saw a yard full of metal sculptures and walked down to meet Fenton Shaw, a 59-year-old metalworker. Fenton had the look of an old hippie and the eccentric art to match. His work was amazing. As we shared our faith with Fenton, he shared his with us. We left the yard full of metal, welded into works of art, rejoicing God had allowed us to enjoy the talent His family possesses.

Thursday, we walked fourteen miles and Friday we walked seventeen. We ended the week with fifty-four miles. Although this was only about half of what we normally accomplished, it was an outstanding victory when the circumstances were considered. We ended the week in Beebe, Arkansas, having chosen to avoid Little Rock and take the shortest route across Arkansas to make up for the lost time. This would be only the second major adjustment to the route planned the year before, and the only major city along our route we would bypass. At the time it seemed like the only possible way to keep our commitment to walking the entire distance and finishing on time. It would prove itself time and time again to be the right decision as we continued to be at exactly the right places at exactly the right times.

We decided to take Saturday off. Our drivers Dick and Bonnie had been with us for the entire month of April. They had been with us through the most stressful month of the walk. They were tired, and I needed a rest. We sent them on their way back to their home in Crossville, Tennessee Saturday morning. We broke camp and moved to Little Rock. I had promised Jane a nice meal and a movie for a belated birthday present. I thought having two days off would do my body good and increase the chances we could get our full mileage in the next week.

Sunday, April 30th was a great day. For the first time since the accident, I was able to wear regular pants and get ready for church. It was a very tentative process to be sure, but I managed to get dressed, drive to Cabot, Arkansas, and have lunch with friends from college, Ken and Lois Holland. Ken was serving First Baptist Church as Associate Pastor of Worship. They had been such wonderful resource people for us during the early days of our traveling ministry and such encouragers to us when we decided to walk across America. The worship service led by Ken was just what the doctor ordered. I left feeling more normal than I had in ten days. Ken and Lois listened to our stories over the homemade pot roast dinner Lois had prepared, and we marveled together how God had blessed in the first seventeen hundred and seventy-eight miles.

We got back to the campground in Little Rock in time to rest a little while before our next driver, Stacy, reported for her second tour of duty. She had also driven for us in New Mexico. As one of the earliest supporters of the walk, she had helped plan the trip. In 2005 she had driven the route from Los Angeles to Oklahoma City, finding the best roads and places to camp along the way. Now she would be with us for a very pivotal and crucial week. What we could accomplish this week would likely determine whether we would make it to Washington by our nation's birthday. We believed God knew all the delays and detours we would end up taking. We had come to trust that if we walked as God directed, and surrendered to His timetable with each step, we would arrive in Washington D.C. by July 4th. And…so we walked.

Chapter 25

Some weeks of the walk were special for reasons all their own. The first full week in May was one of those weeks. The week had its challenges for sure but having a take-charge person like Stacy as our driver was a huge blessing. On Monday the van broke down while Stacy was separated from us by a few miles. Our drivers were rarely behind us on the route, but on this day, Stacy had gone back into town to pick up a few things we needed. Once we found out she was stranded, we either had to walk back to Stacy or keep walking forward and hope she would catch up. We walked forward. By the time Stacy was able to find a repair shop, get towed back to Little Rock, get a ride to the campground to pick up her car and then drive back to where we were walking, five hours had elapsed. This would turn out to be the longest time on the walk when we were without food, water and money. I was still nursing my injuries so to make walking easier; I had left everything I usually carried in the van. Jane had one water bottle to share. It was a scorcher and by the time Stacy finally met us it was 3:00 p.m. We were hot, thirsty and unbelievably hungry. Stacy arrived with supplies, our money and the bad news that our van needed an axle, the first of three we would replace before the end of the walk.

My burns were finally beginning to heal. Taking Saturday and Sunday off had helped. We had recalculated the route to Washington, made a few more minor adjustments in Virginia (decided to stay on the highway instead of hiking part of the Appalachian Trail) and concluded that barring any more delays, we should meet our self-imposed deadline. The biggest obstacle now was money. Monthly pledges were beginning to get unpredictable. One donor who had promised major funding had had financial issues of his own and could not follow through with his commitment. There was less than $1,000 left in our account with a full third of the walk yet to go. Nearly every week brought unexpected expenses like car repairs, and now in the last batch of mail sent from home, we began getting the first of the hospital and doctor bills from my accident. But instead of dwelling on the negatives, we rejoiced in the victories. For the first time in ten days, I was able to walk a full schedule, then another full day. By the end of the week, we had walked 114 miles…a complete week. Somehow, despite the challenges, we had to keep walking.

We would long remember this week as extraordinary because we found ourselves completely engulfed in the African American culture of the south. We were in the minority as we walked by the cotton fields of eastern Arkansas. We waved and called out to untold numbers of black folks who were rocking their hours away on the rickety porches of run-down, bleached-out shanties, leftover, we presumed, from the days of sharecropping. Whether they were walking on the street, loitering in a convenience store parking lot, pumping gas, or working in the garden, the African Americans we met were friendly, receptive and gracious, without exception. No matter how depressed the neighborhood was, how much graffiti was sprayed on the sides of abandoned buildings, or how many people stopped to warn us of danger, we never once felt threatened or afraid. Some of the warmest greetings, tightest hugs and most loving acceptance we experienced on the walk were found in the heart of black America.

There are no words to describe the overwhelming emotions we experienced as we walked among our brothers and sisters of color. We asked God to forgive our nation for the transgressions of our forefathers in the buying and selling of fellow-human beings whose only crime was having skin darker than our own. We were ashamed of our own prejudices that had never surfaced until then. We were humbled in realizing what it must be like to always be in the minority.

The sights and the sounds of this area of our country are unique and extraordinary. There was a constant smell of burning hickory. The ribs, for which Memphis is famous, were slowly being smoked. New and different dialects of the English language could be heard at every place where people gathered. We were exposed to local food preferences, wide smiles, and friendly greetings which made this part of the South one of our favorite places.

It is not possible to properly introduce you to the people we met in West Memphis, Arkansas and Memphis, Tennessee. But if I did not at least attempt to paint a picture of those encounters, I would rob you of much of the meaning of the walk across America. There was Aretha, a black shopkeeper, who invited us in to see her selection of second-hand trinkets and knick-knacks. Most obvious to us were the pictures of Jesus, a black man, surrounded by others like Himself. Her husband was a pastor.

Then there was Ulysses, a toothless, African American man whose head full of hair exploded in all directions from underneath his baseball cap. He was hitch-hiking to town and told us with a huge grin how much he loved Jesus. Mike Morgan was a mountain of a man. His almost-white, three-piece suit and flashy tie accentuated his dark, ebony skin and shaved head. Mike was putting oil in his car and on his way to preach at the funeral of a friend.

Glen had the rough look of someone addicted to alcohol. His friend had just bought him a beer, even though it was still a couple of hours until lunchtime. Glen was visibly moved by our explanation of the walk and said he'd love to walk with us but then added, "I can't because of this," as he held up the can of beer.

Roosevelt Malone was sitting on his front step wearing a bright Hawaiian shirt. Carl had a long scar on the back of his head but said he knew Jesus "100%." Pamela, a short, loud, rotund woman grabbed me before I could stop her. She wrapped her huge, floppy arms around me and buried my astonished face in her bosom. She finally let me up for air exclaiming how happy she was to meet us. Most of the very few white people we saw during these few days were simply passing through neighborhoods on their way to some other, less intimidating place. They cranked their necks around as they drove by, some shaking their heads in disbelief. One woman who was stopped at the corner for a traffic light reluctantly gave us directions from a barely cracked car window and then told us to be careful, in "this neighborhood."

What began in Arkansas and western Tennessee continued throughout the remainder of our days on the road. We had purposefully routed ourselves through inner cities all along the walk without knowing what to expect. We found we were accepted and embraced (literally) much more readily by the poor, the homeless, the African Americans and those who lived in the ghettos, than by those who appeared to be more like us. Our outward differences mattered little to them. What did seem to matter was our open acceptance and determination to treat them with dignity and respect.

I think I have always tried to avoid the pitfalls of prejudice in my life. I am a child of the sixties after all, and many of my childhood heroes like John and Robert Kennedy and Martin Luther King Jr. championed the cause of civil rights. I have hated segregation and discrimination for as long as I can remember. But I can tell you nothing has affected my life as deeply regarding the issue of race as our walk through West Memphis and Memphis. This is where many of the battles for civil rights were fought and the place where Dr. King was assassinated. This is the place where the scars of those battles run deep and where we should have, by all rights, been hated because of the color of our skin. And yet, for whatever reason, we felt comforted as we walked, accepted as we spoke and saddened as we left skid row and headed toward the suburbs. We hesitated several times as we left those neighborhoods and looked back as if to ask ourselves, "Did that really happen?" Four months of experience indicated the affluent would not give us a hearing nearly as quickly as those we had just met. Yet, we knew they too needed to hear the message of love and reconciliation we had just shared with people on the other side of the tracks. Our mission was to walk and pray for all of America. And...so we walked.

Chapter 26

By the second week in May we were closing in on the 2000-mile mark with every step we took. Tennessee is a long state when you walk its width from Memphis to Bristol, but this was the next to the last state and we seemed to be back in our rhythm which had been broken by my accident. Our drivers for the first full week in Tennessee were Norm and Gloria from Saratoga, Wyoming. We had met them while ministering in their home church and when they heard about our walk, they were quick to volunteer.

Gloria was a great encouragement as she walked with us every day. Lots of our drivers tried to walk and keep up but Gloria was one of the few who succeeded. She did get blisters and had to slack off a bit, but when we crossed the 2000-mile mark, Gloria was there. Norm was a great driver. He never got lost, was always where he was supposed to be, and found someone to share the gospel with at almost every stop he made.

Our first day with Norm and Gloria started in Memphis. We had walked the inner-city portion on Saturday the week before and now we were beginning to head out through the remainder of the city and into the suburbs. On Monday we had as many encounters in a single day as any other day of the walk. It was simply amazing. We walked twenty miles, but it took us much longer than normal. There were times when all three of us were carrying on separate conversations at bus stops and in front of stores. We stopped by a donut shop where there was a group of six men gathered around a table drinking coffee and looking at an owner's manual for a backhoe. We kidded with them about the meeting of the "backhoe club" and found they loved Jesus almost as much as they loved heavy machinery.

This would be the rainiest week of the walk. It rained almost every day and we had to sit out for lightning on parts of three days. We just resigned ourselves to God's timing, knowing there was someone ahead we needed to talk to.

We had just started walking again after a short rain delay when the cell phone rang. It was my dad. Our good friend Pat Litton had just passed away after a long fight with cancer. I had been Pat's pastor for several years, Jane and been her piano teacher and she had become one of our dearest church members and friends. This became one of the most difficult parts of the walk. After nearly four and a half months on the road, we had missed surgeries, funerals, birthdays, and other important events because we couldn't take off every time something happened. Everything in us wanted to go home for Pat's funeral, but we knew Pat would want us to keep walking. Pat's death would remind us of something which had kept us going many days when we were discouraged. The book of Hebrews talks about the "great cloud of witnesses." Jane and I began early on to envision that wonderful group of family and friends who had preceded us in death, cheering us on each day as we walked. Jane's father was there and her grandparents. All my grandparents and so many of our friends were there too. It may seem strange, but I believe there were days when we simply could not have finished our miles had we not had that vision to fall back on.

Jane and I have always been common people. We've never had a lot of money or worldly riches. We've never attained much notoriety or fame. I think that's one reason why we were always surprised when strangers seemed to know us. Many times, walking down a road or highway, people would wave and honk or even pull over to talk with us because they had seen us on TV or heard about us on the radio. It was incredible how many times we would go into a convenience store and people would say, "We saw you on the news last night." Lots of times we didn't even know we'd been on the news.

We really have no idea how many websites, blogs, radio stations, newspapers and television newscasts told our story. We sent out information to a national newswire service every few weeks. Once the story got out on the wire services, it spread all over the country. One of the byproducts of that kind of publicity turned out to be one of our greatest blessings: The constant prayers that were being offered up for us in churches all over the country. One day our drivers, Norm and Gloria, found a little store owned by a Mennonite family. The next time they met us for a break they said, "You've got to come meet this family." We drove back to the little store and went inside. The man behind the counter said, "We talked about you in our church last Sunday and then we prayed for you." What are the chances a Mennonite church would hear our story and pray for us the Sunday before we happened to be walking through their town and stop at their store? This happened time and again confirming God's care for us and reminding us He had not forgotten us. Although there were naysayers and skeptics within the churches along the way, there also seemed to be those whose spirits identified with ours and the burden we felt for America. Without regard to denomination or background, God would intersect our path with someone who encouraged us and joined with us in praying for our nation.

McDonald's® became one of our favorite stops. Although we seldom ate there, we could always count on them for nice, clean restrooms. We also tried to keep $5 McDonald's® gift cards tucked away to give to those who were homeless and hungry, so stopping there gave us an opportunity to replenish our supply. I wish we had kept track of how many gift cards we gave away, just out of curiosity, but I'm sure it represented hundreds of meals for those who were hungry.

During one of those stops as we approached middle Tennessee, we met a group of several high school students sitting at a table with a man who looked old enough to be their father. When we greeted them, we asked them why they weren't in school. They told us they were on a field trip with their teacher. We found it all very suspicious and wondered why our teachers had never taken us to McDonald's® on a field trip. It gave us a wonderful opportunity to tell them about our own little field trip and to ask them about their spiritual condition. It was great to share with them and find they were all followers of Christ.

Those McDonald's® gift cards were purchased, almost entirely, with money people gave us along the way. It amazed us how generous people were, even though we were strangers. People gave us money, sometimes as little as two one-dollar bills, crumbled and worn almost in half. Other people gave us free drinks and food at their stores or took us out to eat. Churches, who sometimes didn't know we were coming, provided for our needs. When needed, they even found volunteers to drive for us on short notice. Several times people filled up our vehicles with gas which sometimes represented a gift of nearly $200. Every time someone gave us cash, Jane always put it in her little pouch and saved it for giving away.

Early in the walk we noticed there were coins every so often on the road or the shoulder beside the road. We started picking up the change and always saved it separately from all the other money. Each day we put it away and continued to do this for the entire journey. Most of the coins were pennies and nickels, but sometimes there were dimes and quarters too. We decided not to count it until the end of the walk at which time we discovered we had picked up over $75 in loose change. We gave it all to a very special ministry in Washington D.C. that had been supportive of our walk.

Although it would have been tempting to keep what was given to us along the way and even the change we found, we held on to a biblical principle we believed with all our hearts. We believed if we would continue to give away what God put in our hands, He would make sure we had all we needed. We saw that principle work repeatedly as we neared the bottom of our resources and had to count on Him for His.

This principle applied not only to financial resources but to other needs as well. As the week ended, we did not have a driver for the following week. We would be walking into Nashville and desperately needed a driver. There had been only two days up until this point when we had to walk without a driver. Because this would mean cutting our mileage in half each day, it would be the fatal blow to getting to Washington on time. We put out one final plea on the website for a driver. That evening the phone rang. It was Pastor Ron Teed from Wheaton, IL. He and his wife had driven for us in Arizona and New Mexico. He would be willing to take a week off and come drive for us if we needed him. God had provided once again proving what we already knew to be true: You cannot outgive God.

Meanwhile, despite rain, lightning, narrow roads with lots of trucks, the death of our dear friend Pat and dwindling finances, the week with Norm and Gloria was amazing. We shared our story, the story of the walk, the story of our Savior and the stories of His provision with everyone we met. Near the end of the week, as we walked down an isolated back road still wet from a recent downpour, we were approached by a man who was leaning as he walked. The tall, friendly, black man smiled with a crooked smile. We stopped to shake his hand and he introduced himself in haltering words. "I'm Jackie Bush," he slurred in response to our outstretched hands. "Jackie, do you know Jesus?" Jane asked. Through his crooked smile, he answered, "Yes, ma'am. Yes ma'am, I do." As we talked to Jackie for a few minutes we found he had had a stroke in 1993 and had been in the hospital for two years and nine months. Now he walks two miles every day.

God gave us the opportunity to meet many people who had overcome and were persevering through much greater physical, emotional and financial challenges than we were facing. Part of the mission was to encourage them in their daily walk. Jackie Bush was one of those people. Jane encouraged him by reminding him God had preserved him for a purpose. He agreed. But Jackie had a purpose that day too. He was there on that lonely, hot, humid Tennessee backroad to encourage two people who had heard God say, "Walk across America." If Jackie could walk…so could we. And…so we walked.

Chapter 27

One of the lessons God taught us on a very deep level during the walk was how interdependent the body is. The physical body is an amazing creation, but to some degree, each body part's function is dependent on the other part's ability to perform satisfactorily. Jane, for example, had to alter the way she walked because of her blisters. Walking toe first or favoring the sides of her feet to avoid putting the full weight of her body on the blisters affected all the other parts of her body. When one part of the body has to compensate for a weakness in another part, it affects the whole. Even when my finger was in a splint and my arm in a sling, my ability to walk freely and efficiently was diminished.

There is a paramount spiritual lesson in this physical example. The body of Christ is also interdependent. Although we like to think we are spiritually independent and that only our own obedience matters, the truth is that when other parts of His body are not obedient, it does affect our ability to function as He planned. Grasping this truth would add a whole new dimension to our spiritual journey.

Picture, for example, a jigsaw puzzle. My dad loved jigsaw puzzles and every Christmas for many years, regardless of what else he received, he always got at least one puzzle. There was rarely a time during my childhood when there wasn't a half-finished puzzle somewhere in the house. I did not inherit my father's patience for tedious puzzle work. My tendency was to find a piece that almost fit and force it into place. Dad would always shake his head and gently remove the ill-fitting piece and replace it with the right one. "Now, that's better," he'd say. "But Dad, I got it to fit," I'd protest. Then Dad would show me the difference between a perfect fit and a "forced" fit. The forced fit always left little gaps and affected the picture's beauty.

Although we were extremely grateful for Ron, our fill-in driver for the week, we became more aware every day it may have been the case of a forced fit. This is absolutely no reflection on Ron. On the contrary, Ron is to be commended for picking up the dropped baton and running a leg of the race he probably wasn't supposed to run. Sometimes filling in is the best we can do when others don't listen or don't obey God's instruction. Ron compensated for a part of the body that didn't function properly and for that, we will be forever grateful.

But it became evident early in the week that things were just off. Nothing worked right. On Monday the motel desk didn't give Ron his wake-up call. When we arrived to pick Ron up, he was still in bed, sound asleep (Ron had driven from Chicago to Nashville after church on Sunday morning). We took the van in for routine service and ended up with another new axle (that made two), and a crushed oil pan (they left the jack under the car when they lowered the lift). The only rental car was a pick-up truck which meant all our supplies, first-aid kit, food and portable toilet were all in the van which would be in the repair shop for two days. I got horribly sick with chills, fever, upset stomach and dizziness. I lived on 7-Up® and very little else for three days. We talked to almost no one until we got to Nashville. We withdrew the last of our money from our account and the few hundred dollars I now had in my wallet was all there was. The weather was dreary and rainy all week and to be honest Jane and I both had lousy attitudes. We were ready to be done with this whole thing.

Then, to add to the troubles of the week, just outside of Nashville on an isolated country road, I had an allergic reaction to something in the air. My windpipe began to close off and I couldn't breathe. I panicked and started to cry out for help. Jane tried to calm me down, but I couldn't breathe...I thought I was going to die! Jane tried to call 911 but we had no cell service. I drank water, trying to flush the pollen or whatever it was from my throat. Finally, after several very tense minutes, the airway seemed to open a bit and I could breathe. I learned later from a nurse that my reaction could have been deadly. It was scary and seemed to put an exclamation mark at the end of a very frustrating week. It was becoming glaringly obvious that the enemy did not want us to finish this walk.

What had happened? Well, to be sure some of it was self-imposed. Our attitudes were our fault. No one else was responsible. And the weather? We couldn't control that nor could anyone else. The car repairs, my sickness, and the lack of people may have all been beyond our control. But we wondered if things would have been different if someone else was supposed to be our driver that week and didn't accept the assignment. What if someone different would have been driving and had taken the van to a different repair shop? What if that person had been an extreme encourager who would have helped us check our attitudes and get back on track? What if the driver had pulled over to wait in different locations spawning different encounters? Was it Ron's fault? Absolutely not. Had he not filled the hole in the puzzle the best he could, it would have left a gap in the walk and affected everything else down the line. The body carried on...compensating for a missing part...it walked... but it walked with a limp.

We have no idea who may have been called to drive that week. We do know God used us despite our attitudes and we finished the week, even with all the issues, with 109 miles. We did speak to people about Christ, and we did see His hand in the encounters we had. Our time with Ron was precious and his willingness to serve us and serve others along the way was a wonderful testimony of God's Spirit in him. Our concern was not for us or Ron. Ultimately, we were obedient and accomplished what God called us to do. Our concern was for the missed lessons and blessings which could have been received by the person who may have been the missing piece of the puzzle. Some of our drivers were radically changed by their being a part of the walk. Could there have been another person whose direction in life could have been altered, their relationship with the Lord revitalized, or their calling reinforced? We may never know, but it does make me consider something about my own life. I've wondered many times since the walk about times in my life when I may have missed what God had for me by not being where I was supposed to be at the right time. I don't think God withholds things to be mean, and I don't think he holds a grudge. I do believe it's possible to miss the abundance of blessings He intends for us to enjoy when we are where we want to be instead of where He's called us to be.

There was one very special blessing during this week. Jane and I had left our hometown on Christmas Day 2005 to drive to Los Angeles. I had not seen my parents for four and a half months. Mom and Dad drove to Nashville to spend a week while we were camping there. The first night we stopped to see them I was so sick and weak that I simply collapsed on the sofa. Mom wrapped me up in a blanket because I was chilling and fixed me hot tea. Each night after the walk we stopped by for a few minutes and later in the week when I felt better, we went out to eat. Our visits with them increased the length of the day, but it was a wonderful treat to be with family.

The feeling of isolation we felt many days after walking was oppressive. There were days when human contact was minimal and even when there were conversations, they were not the kind with real intimate sharing; the kind which feeds your soul. Some drivers were friends or became friends on the walk, but even those conversations were brief while we changed our shoes or grabbed a fresh water bottle.

Having Mom and Dad there was refreshing. It drew attention to the fact the walk had become a parallel universe of sorts, completely separated from our home, our family and our friends.

During the walk, my family back home had begun to notice some health issues with Mom. She was getting confused, had problems driving and was exhibiting some strange behavior. Mom had beaten cancer several times, but now was exhibiting new symptoms which were unsettling to the family. This made the reunion with Mom and Dad in Nashville much more special. After spending time with them, I only hoped they would be well enough to meet us in Washington D.C.

One of the nice things about walking in late spring in the South was so many people were out in their yards working, or alongside the road in make-shift fruit stands selling produce from their gardens, or manning garage sales that spilled out onto the sidewalk. It gave us plenty of opportunities to share in and around Nashville. There was Jerry cutting limbs in his yard after a storm had blown them down. He said he knew Jesus. Then we met James and Louise at a roadside stand where we bought sweet corn and watermelon. James hoped he was "ready." We prayed he would know for sure. Then there was Joyce, who appeared to be blind in one eye, a man getting his mail out of the mailbox who acted like he'd had too much to drink, and a homeless man to whom we gave a McDonald's® gift card and then helped buy a prescription he needed. Even wrong numbers along the way were used to share the love of Christ. Someone called our toll-free number as we were walking through Nashville. She thought she had dialed the phone company. I'm not sure why, but I said, "You've got the wrong number, but while I've got you on the phone do you mind if I ask you a question? Do you know Jesus?"

One of the best things about walking through Tennessee was the plentiful news coverage, especially on TV. The Nashville ABC affiliate came out to interview and videotape us as we walked. Whenever we were on TV, people would honk and wave for several days after the broadcast as we walked through their city. While walking through Nashville, we got a real treat. We rounded a corner downtown not long after we started walking for the day. We couldn't help but notice the loud rap music blaring from a concrete block building that had been converted into a full-service car wash. There he was, the king of the car wash, with his oversized, saggy jeans and baseball hat cocked slightly off-center. At his beck and call were three or four young black women in cut-off short shorts and tight tank tops. They were soaping up the car to the beat of the music and honestly, if I hadn't known better, I would have thought we had stepped onto the set of a very funny movie. As soon as Mr. Car Wash saw us, he started toward us and half-shouted to be heard over the music, "Hey, didn't I see you dudes on the TV last night?" His gold tooth glistened in the morning sun. "You may have. We're the ones walking across America," I responded. The power of the television coverage was amazing. We had a wonderful opportunity to share with all the car wash employees. They even wanted our autograph on our card.

When we started planning the walk in early 2005, we had no idea what kind of people we would meet. We met every kind of person imaginable. We met or talked to hundreds of homeless people. We talked to people who could not have afforded a cheap cup of coffee. On the other hand, we met and were introduced to people who could have bought a dozen Starbucks® franchises and never blinked an eye. God gave us favor with people of all races, all economic backgrounds, all political parties and all kinds of religious and denominational preferences. Something about the walk transcended all the things which usually divide us. It was one of the unanticipated highlights of the whole adventure.

One interesting side note: There were no political overtones to the walk. However, it was interesting how most people assumed there was. In states where many of the people we talked to probably leaned toward the liberal side of politics, they assumed we were conservative (probably because of the faith element). One lady near Flagstaff, Arizona didn't want anything to do with us (she wouldn't even take a card) because she was sure the walk across America was a "Bush thing." In other places where people tended to be more conservative, they assumed we were liberal (maybe because walking across America is something only old hippies would do). Reporters couldn't figure us out either because we didn't fit any of the Christian stereotypes they had. It was fun to keep people guessing. Part of the goal was to cause others to rethink their preconceived notions about what a follower of Christ really looked like. In that regard, the walk was a huge success.

Ron had saved us from a week without a driver. It had been a rough week in a lot of ways, and we wondered if we could get back on track. Mom and dad's visit had helped, and I was finally feeling better by the end of the week. We walked through the heart of Nashville, past the old Ryman Theater, down music row and out toward the Cumberland Plateau. We ended the week in Lebanon, Tennessee home of Cracker Barrel® restaurants. We had gotten a call on Friday from some friends of Ken and Lois Holland back in Cabot, Arkansas. They lived in Tennessee and heard about the walk. They wanted to come meet us on Saturday. When they arrived, they took Ron back to his car in Nashville, so he could start back to Chicago. Then they drove ahead and waited for us at, where else but Cracker Barrel®. Mike and Ann Johnson treated us to a wonderful lunch and gave us a Cracker Barrel® gift card and a check for $200. It would take a while for the check to be mailed back home, clear the bank as an out-of-state check and be accessible to us, but if we could hang on financially until then, it would sure come in handy. After lunch, the Johnsons took us out to the truck stop where our camper and van were parked. We filled up with gas and drove onto the Interstate. The next stop would be the KOA in Crossville, Tennessee.

The hills were tough on the old camper which had rolled over 100,000 miles on the walk. I should have waited to fill both vehicles up with gas until we were past the steep grades, as that added hundreds of pounds in fuel to the load, but it was too late now. The temperature gauge was getting closer and closer to the red zone with every hill we climbed. Finally, when it crossed the line, I decided to pull into a rest stop and let the engine rest and cool down.

We were so close to finishing the walk. We were halfway across Tennessee, and we'd be in Virginia by the first week in June. It looked like our bodies were going to allow us to punish them for a few more weeks. Surely, if we could walk it, the vehicles would hold out. And if we were able to walk the last 650 miles or so, wouldn't the money come through, so we could make it to Washington? I just kept remembering the words to the old song, "He didn't bring us this far to leave us. He didn't teach us to swim to let us drown." How I hoped that was right.

I turned the key just enough to see where the temperature gauge was registering. Back to normal…good. We decided to unhook the van from the camper to lighten the load for the last few miles. We drove separately into the campground, registered and talked with Sherry, the manager. We told her the story of the walk, she shared she was a Believer and she promised to alert her friends to pray for us. As we were getting ready to leave the office, I noticed a piano in the back room and asked if I could play it. My finger was now out of the splint, but I still could not bend it at all. I had not tried to play since the accident. I was very tentative as I placed my hands on the keyboard. I played. I played around the stiff finger, and improvised the fingering, but I played. It was unbelievably emotional for me. One of my greatest fears after the accident was that I wouldn't be able to play the piano again. Now I knew I could. It may never be quite the same, and the finger may never work exactly right, but I could play. Tears rolled down Jane's face as she watched. I know she was remembering that awful morning and the depressing prognosis of the doctor who wasn't sure I'd ever use my finger to play the piano or guitar again. No one else could possibly have understood the emotion of those moments at the keyboard except us. God had once again been victorious over the circumstances. Oh, how I hoped He would come through in one more very important matter.

We set up camp and got ready to rest. I didn't want to tell Jane what I needed to tell her, but I knew I had no choice. She could always tell when bad news was coming, and I could sense her internally brace herself for what I was getting ready to say. "I just used the last two $100 bills to pay the camping fee for this week. We have the change and that's all there is," I said looking down at the thirty-some dollars in my hand.

Jane never flinched as she responded, "We'll walk as far as we can this week and when we need to move, God will provide." It was that simple for Jane. All my worrying and figuring things out on paper never rattled her. The black and white of the ledger sheet never shook her faith in the black and white promises on the pages of God's Word. There was no fear or regret in her voice. We would obey God and He would honor His promises. We would walk as long as we could. And…so we walked.

Chapter 28

On Sunday we worshipped with the small congregation of New Hope Baptist Church. They met in a room at a local motel. Their pastor, Vern Daugherty had become a dear friend. We had met Pastor Vern a few years earlier when going door to door, calling on churches to introduce our evangelistic ministry. We had ministered to the small, mostly senior adult congregation several times and were glad to see them again. We shared about the walk and they gave us a small offering, perhaps enough to buy food and gas for the van for the week.

Our driver for the week was Brother Howard Whiteley from Baxter Springs, Kansas. He and his wife were another couple who had become dear to us over our years of ministry on the road. Because of other obligations, he could not start driving until Tuesday, so Monday we had a one-day driver. We met George back in Nashville, Tennessee at Two Rivers Baptist Church. George was a vibrant Christian businessman who was really interested in the walk and gave us his card. He said if we needed anything to let him know. We called to see if he could drive for us, and he agreed. So, on Monday we drove the van back to Lebanon to meet George and begin walking east once again. At our first rest break, George told us the van really needed some work (one of George's businesses was an auto repair shop). He arranged for us to take in the van that evening and get new tires and some other work done. He volunteered to pay the entire bill. Just after lunch, we were walking out in the country. Suddenly, a sharp pain stabbed me in the leg. It felt like someone had taken an ice pick or sharp knife and jammed it into the side of my leg just above the knee. I cried out in pain. Jane turned around and thought I was having a heart attack or something. It hurt so much I could not control the spontaneous cry. It was gone as fast as it came but I never wanted to feel that pain again. A few miles down the road it hit again. Again, I cried out. I had never been shot with a gun, but if I were trying to imagine what it would feel like to have a bullet rip through my body, this pain was exactly what I would have expected. What was it? I had walked over 2100 miles. Why now? Then, I remembered the fall I took on the day of the accident. The burns and my injured finger had taken priority. No one (including us) had thought about the fall very much. I had had a limp for a few days and my lower back hurt, but this wasn't my back…it was my leg. I had noticed when I went to bed each night, I had to hold my leg bent so it didn't hurt. Was this all connected? I had no way of knowing now, and a doctor and X-rays were completely out of the question. There was no money.

    At the end of the day, I think I was in shock. How could I finish the walk with this pain? We drove to Murfreesboro, Tennessee where George's repair shop was located. We got there at 5:30 p.m. and they worked on the van until almost 8:00 p.m. which was our normal bedtime. While we were waiting on the van, we received our weekly call from the prayer team back home. Every week of the walk, they met together to pray for our needs and for the ministry which was taking place with each mile we walked. They never missed a week. They always ended the conversation of encouragement with and prayer on speakerphone. Many times, I would hold our little flip phone up to Jane's ear, so we could both hear them praying for us. When the conversation was over, we got in the van and drove the long drive back to Crossville. It was nearly 10:00 p.m. when we got in bed, but we were thankful. The van had new tires and fresh oil and it hadn't cost us a thing.

The next morning Brother Whiteley greeted us as we stepped out of the camper. His white hair and ear-to-ear grin were a welcome sight. Good friends have a way of making the day seem brighter. His presence made us feel like everything was going to be alright. Maybe yesterday's leg pain was just a fluke. We loaded up and drove back to our starting point. Yesterday we had only walked 17 miles…three miles short. Today we would need to do better. The hills of middle Tennessee are not mountains, but they are a challenge for tired walkers. The two-lane roads were narrow, curvy and either up or down, almost never flat. We also noticed another unwelcome sight, dogs. Not just any dogs. These were watchdogs that ran loose protecting the territory of their owners. Many were pit bulls and when we walked anywhere near the perimeter of their domain, they were not happy. One of our early drivers, Cliff, was a letter carrier for the Post Office. He had sent some government issue dog spray to carry just in case. We really didn't want to use the spray, but I always had it with me. On numerous occasions, a dog would be in attack mode and headed toward us when the owner would stick their head out of a backwoods cabin and call the dog. We would gingerly walk on by, our hearts pounding in our throats, wondering what would have happened if the dog's owner had not been home.

On Brother Whiteley's first day, we walked 21 miles, but not on purpose. We were supposed to walk 20 miles, a full day's schedule. The problem was there were no pull-offs for him to wait beside the road. When he was finally able to find a place, he had driven an extra mile. Let me remind you; a driven mile is much different from a walked one, especially after walking 20 miles. Every time we went around another hairpin turn, we expected to see the van waiting for us. Not there. Another turn. Not there. By the time we finally saw the van, I was ready to wring someone's neck (not necessarily Brother Whiteley's neck. Anyone's neck would have been fine). It's a good thing one of those dogs didn't come after me late that afternoon. The dog wouldn't have stood a chance!

By the way, even with all the most positive of thoughts and encouragement from our wonderful driver Brother Whiteley, my leg pain continued off and on throughout the day. As a matter of fact, every day for the rest of the walk, with no warning at all, I would cry out in pain. Sometimes two or three times a day, sometimes a dozen. There was no way to prevent it, although wearing a tight elastic bandage around my leg sometimes seemed to lessen the intensity. We began to rate the day by how many times I cried out in pain. Three or less was a good day. I had always been adamant about driving the van back to camp at the end of the day. I have never enjoyed being a passenger. But I found it was dangerous to drive. If my leg had one of the painful spasms while I was driving, I wasn't sure what would happen. I reluctantly began letting the driver for the day drive us back each evening. A few months later, after the walk was over, I would discover I had pinched a nerve when I fell the day of the accident. The pinched nerve was connected somehow to my leg muscle. The pain took much of the joy out of walking. I was in survival mode. We were so close to finishing, but the pain was almost unbearable. For the first time in over 2,000 miles, I became the weak link. No amount of pain, however, could take the joy out of sharing the love of Jesus with those we encountered.

Sharing on the back roads of Tennessee was quite a contrast from the city streets of Memphis and Nashville. When you walked in the country, your encounters came at gas stations, convenience stores, or roadside parks along scenic highways. Sometimes you walked five or ten miles between people. That created a lot of in-between time. Many people have asked what we did during the hundreds of hours we spent walking when there were no people. We prayed, sang, talked and prayed some more. This kept us ready to share and our spirits sensitive when we came upon those divine appointments.

We chose to believe every encounter was orchestrated by God. We believed His timing was perfect and what appeared to be chance meetings were providential. We climbed a hill one day and there was a group of four or five construction workers just standing there as if they were waiting for us to arrive. They acted as though they were in a stupor. When we walked up, they snapped out of it and we had the opportunity to share the gospel with them. Another day we came upon a wreck that had just happened in front of a convenience store. It gave us a perfect opportunity to share a prayer with the young woman who had collided with a utility pole. Sometimes when people heard our story, they would ask us to pray for something in their life. The need could be anything. Sometimes it was a son or daughter in trouble or a family member serving in Iraq or relationship problems in the marriage of a friend or neighbor. It was amazing how people opened up to perfect strangers just because we were walking across America. And…so we walked.

Chapter 29

The four days with Brother Whitely were uneventful except for the two separate occasions when he was awakened out of a sound sleep to be questioned by police about being pulled off the road in front of someone's house. Apparently, people in Tennessee are suspicious of white-haired men with out-of-state plates who park for long periods of time in front of their homes. If the police had only known how strait-laced Brother Whitely really was, they would have let the poor man sleep.

There were dozens of encounters that week which we would categorize as normal. But then on Friday afternoon something would happen that was definitely out of the ordinary. We were parked under a huge maple tree after our first twelve or thirteen miles. We had just started eating lunch when the cell phone rang. It was a man from Faith Bible Fellowship in Fairfield Glade, Tennessee where we were scheduled to speak on Sunday morning. Jane and I had ministered at this wonderful, small fellowship several times and had come to love their Pastor and his wife, David and Linda Evangelista. The man on the other end of the phone had a strange question. "How much money do you need to finish the walk?" he asked. I was flustered, to say the least, and the truth was I wasn't sure. I had assumed we would limp our way into Washington D.C., financially speaking, because our money was gone for all intents and purposes and there were precious few promises for anymore. I was embarrassed I didn't really know but I quickly calculated the number of weeks left and multiplied it by the bare minimum we could live on each week. I came up with about three thousand dollars. I was reluctant to even say it. Was it presumptuous to mention such a large sum? Surely, he wasn't asking because he had access to that kind of money. I timidly gave the figure of three thousand dollars and immediately felt like a fool. I quickly qualified my calculations explaining that "some may come in over the next few days…maybe it wouldn't take that much…I'm sure we'll be fine."

As I closed my flip phone, I wasn't sure whether to cry for joy or despair. If he meant they were going to try to raise what we needed, I should be happy. If the small congregation raised even a portion, it would be a huge help in getting us down the road a little further. The sad part was, for the first time I had put hard, cold calculations to the remaining days of the walk and realized we were three thousand dollars short. I had not really let myself think about it much. It was depressing to know the amount of the shortfall. I tried to imagine how we could save on expenses: We could camp in Walmart parking lots to cut camping expenses, we could change our eating habits some (although we had to eat enough to have the strength to walk), and we could cut a few corners here and there, but we really were going to need most of three thousand dollars to finish the walk. I shared the nature of the phone call with Jane, and we agreed all our thinking and worrying wouldn't change the bottom line: God would somehow help us finish what He led us to begin.

Sunday morning, we got up and got ready for church. We were a little nervous because we didn't know what to expect. On the one hand, we didn't want to expect too much and be disappointed. On the other hand, we wanted to believe God was going to provide for our needs. We wondered if He may just use this group of senior adults living in a retirement community to do it.

After the congregation sang a few hymns, Jane and I were called to the front to share our experiences on the walk thus far. We showed pictures and told the stories of lives God had allowed us to touch as we walked one step at a time across America. At the end of the service, we were presented with an envelope that contained two checks. The first was for $3000, enough to finish the walk. The second check was for $1000. God had done it; he had provided for the remainder of the trip. We had not known until this moment that the walk across America would end up fully funded. Jane and I had done everything humanly possible to raise the funds. We had sold truckloads full of our personal belongings in yard sales and flea markets. We had emptied our house, put our remaining things in storage, and put our house on the market hoping to sell it to have money for the walk. Friends, family, and churches had given sacrificially, many times. Even strangers had written notes of encouragement with small checks tucked in to help make the walk possible. On one occasion, just before the walk began, we were asked to drive six hundred miles to a tiny church in Taneyville, Missouri. "New Beginnings Full Gospel Church," where we had ministered several times, wanted us to come on a Wednesday night. Although it was a long drive, the pastor, Austin Sutton and his wife Shirley convinced us to come and said it would be worth our while. Wednesday night we shared with the congregation our conviction God had called us to walk across America. At the end of the service, they asked Jane and me to stand at the front of the very old building that literally leaned to one side. While we held what began as an empty basket, the fifth and sixth graders got up from their seats and dropped change, and small denomination dollar bills into the basket. By the time they had all come forward, there was over $1,000 dollars in the basket. They had held rummage sales, bake sales, raffles and car washes to raise the money to purchase our shoes. The money deposited in the basket that night was the actual money raised, the very dollar bills which had been collected by this group of young people. We stood and wept as they came one at a time and gave their offerings of love. That gift paid for over half of the twenty pairs of shoes we would wear while walking from coast to coast.

We saw God provide over and over, but He had never cut it quite so close as in Crossville, Tennessee. Our funds were depleted and there was nowhere else to draw from except God's bounty, but His bounty is always enough. The four thousand dollars went into the mail to be deposited in our account on Monday morning. Now money was not an issue. If Jane's feet and my legs could walk the remaining miles, if there were no more accidents, if there were no big repairs to the van or camper, if we could secure volunteer drivers for the last few weeks, and could conquer the mountains of east Tennessee and Virginia in a timely fashion (a lot of ifs), we might just make it to the Supreme Court building by July 4th.

Volunteer drivers were getting scarce. There were about five weeks left in the walk with no solid commitments to drive. We had resorted to using some one-day drivers, which was usually difficult. But sometimes it was fun, like when we had a couple of happy

Pentecostal women who drove for us one Saturday in Tennessee. They laughed and giggled all day. They even sang to us as we approached the van each time for a break. On the other hand, we had a driver who got completely lost from us the next Saturday. We had to recruit some strangers to go find him and get him to return to where we were. We had become separated on a divided highway with tall pines down the middle. He couldn't see us, and we didn't see him. It's scary when you lose your almost eighty-year-old driver on a Saturday afternoon.

By this point in the walk, most of our friends and family who were available had already driven. Some, like Ron and Stacy, had already given a second week. We pulled out all the stops and made a desperate cry for a few more drivers. Two more family members volunteered to drive, my sister Susan and Jane's sister Brenda. A friend of another driver from the Chicago area, whom we did not know, and two more friends from our home church rounded out the trip. In all, we had about thirty different drivers. Some were better than others. Some we wanted to kiss by the end of the day and some we wanted to…well, never mind. Our drivers made the walk across America possible. Not only did they keep in contact with us every three or four miles throughout the day, carry water, food and first aid supplies, drive us back and forth to the starting points and campground each morning and evening, and keep careful records of every mile we walked, but they also became our single connection to the outside world and helped maintain some degree of sanity during those six months of walking. During the time we were walking, little else in the world registered. We heard little news and were isolated from most current events. The drivers were our only link to the "real" world.

It's hard to believe people would give up a week and in a couple of cases, multiple weeks to drive for us without pay or compensation of any kind. They put up with our irritability and complaining, tried to follow explicit directions and still stay available for ministry as they sat for many hours along the road waiting for us. We tried in our own way to honor them and thank them for their servant-like heart, but nothing could ever convey the gratitude we have for them.

Just about the time we thought we'd seen everything on the walk, something or someone would surprise us. Such was the case as we walked between Crossville and Knoxville, Tennessee. On Memorial Day, John Milligan, who was 78 years old, wanted to walk with us. John was in good health and hiked a few miles each month with a hiking club. He felt he could do the entire twenty miles. It was very hot, upper 90's, and extremely humid. By mid-morning John was looking flushed and we were concerned for him. He made it until our lunch break and we fully expected him to drop out for the afternoon. But after lunch, John got up and started walking again. By mid-afternoon, we looked back, and John was staggering a bit. We encouraged him to stop, but he was determined to finish the day. You really can't argue with a 78-year-old man, by the way. Anyway, John finished the day. Every step…all twenty miles…simply amazing. We treated John to an ice cream cone but were forced to reconsider letting someone with relatively little long-distance walking experience tag along in the future. We would have just felt horrible if something had happened to John.

By contrast, we had a group come down from a Christian School in Ohio. We had held an assembly in the school before the walk and they had been praying for us each day. They thought it would be awesome to take a field trip to Tennessee and walk with us one afternoon. The kids did well and most of them walked three or four miles. The adults mostly dropped out after a mile or so. It was interesting to see the 80-year-old walk so far, and others so little. Just like with Jane and me, it had everything to do with calling and determination.

Knoxville would be one of the last large cities until Washington D.C. As was our custom, we chose a path that would take us directly through the most inner-city areas of Knoxville. We loved the sights, sounds and smells of urban areas and loved meeting the people who lived downtown on the streets. We began meeting homeless people sleeping on park benches at Santa Monica Pier on the first day of the walk, but soon realized the homeless were everywhere. We met them on or near the Native American Reservations when we walked near Interstate bridges, and in the back alleys of Amarillo, Oklahoma City, Memphis and Nashville. As we walked through Knoxville the homeless were propped up against old buildings where they had slept the night before. There we met Reba Jean. She was clean, her hair combed and if we had met her under different circumstances, we would not have assumed she was homeless. Reba Jean shared a familiar story. She wanted to work, and had put in hundreds of applications, but because she had no home address or phone number, employers were reluctant to hire her. It's understandable from a business owner's perspective. You need to be able to get in touch with your employees for schedule changes and emergencies. It's also reasonable for potential employers to have a concern about hiring a person who has made the kinds of decisions that may have led to their homelessness. But you could also hear the hopelessness in Reba Jean's voice, knowing her chances of becoming a productive, employed citizen were extremely slim. She couldn't get a phone and apartment without a job, and she couldn't get a job without a phone and home address. We wondered how many of the homeless across America desire to work and would work if they had a legitimate way of providing phone numbers and addresses to prospective employers. There are no easy answers to the problem of homelessness. Some of it is the result of alcoholism and drug addiction, but not all of it. Some is the result of bad decision-making, but not all. There are many homeless who find themselves without a home or shelter by little or no fault of their own. Circumstances have been unkind to some of them and nothing they do will likely be able to pull them out of the gutters and back alleyways. Throwing money at the problem of homelessness, or even at the homeless themselves, is not a long-term solution. We wondered: What would happen if the Church became engaged in a process of rescue, education, mentoring and investing time in the homeless to bring about long-term solutions to the problem?

We did not have the time or resources to make much difference in the life of Reba Jean. She probably doesn't even remember meeting a couple of people who were walking across America. But God used people like Reba Jean to burden our hearts and motivate us to lead the Church to find solutions for those who are homeless. Walking gave us eyes to see the homeless and a heart to care for them. And…so we walked.

Chapter 30

One of the lessons we learned during these six months was the special significance we placed on certain days. In one way, every day was the same. Every morning, long before sunrise, we got out of bed and began preparations for a day of walking twenty or so miles. The scenery changed, and the names of the people changed, but in some ways, every day was a replay of the previous day. As the walk progressed, it got harder and harder to remember the particulars. Days and details all started running together.

In another way, there were those special days of significance that brought reality back into focus and forced us to remember that days were passing, the miles really were moving us toward our goal and regardless of how far removed from our previous life we seemed to be separated, we weren't living in a bubble or time capsule. We were still the same people we had always been. It may sound strange, but even now, the whole experience of walking across America seems surreal and slightly out of focus like a dream.

One of those special days was June 7th, our anniversary. We could not afford, mileage-wise, to take a day off. Every day was now of great importance and given what we now knew about unexpected delays, we didn't dare relax and enjoy our 32nd anniversary by not walking. We camped for the week in the Kingsport, Tennessee/Bristol, Virginia area. The campground sent around a flyer about the availability of take-out ribs. Jane loves ribs, and so our anniversary celebration consisted of ordering ribs and eating them in our camper that evening after walking twenty miles. It may not sound like much of a treat, but honestly, being pulled back to the reality of the calendar was refreshing. We had now been walking for over five months. We had trudged across California, Nevada, Arizona, New Mexico, Texas, Oklahoma, Arkansas and the granddaddy of them all, Tennessee. This long narrow state accounted for nearly five hundred miles of our journey. On our anniversary, we crossed into Bristol, Virginia on foot. This was our last state. We had now walked 2,388 miles. There were less than four hundred to go. This day, June 7th was pivotal. If we could walk one hundred miles per week for the next four weeks, we would make it to Washington D.C. by the Fourth of July. However, there were some obstacles. Even though we had enough money, and enough time (assuming we could continue our twenty-miles per-day pace), our bodies were getting weaker every day. Jane's blisters continued to make walking nearly impossible. My leg pain was so great that nearly every step caused a stabbing pain that radiated from my hip to my knee. Our walking speed was getting slower, the hills were some of the steepest of the entire walk, and although we could not imagine giving up at this point, we wondered every day about our ability to keep going. It dawned on us that what we had asked our bodies to do was to walk 75-80% of a full marathon, every day, 5-6 days every week, for over five months. There was no time for our muscles and joints to recover. We wondered if one day our bodies would simply shut down and say, "No more!" If that day was coming, we prayed it would be sometime after we reached our destination.

    Most days, the prospect of meeting someone on the road was the only thing that kept us going. If God had gone to all the trouble to set up divine appointments with those who needed a word of encouragement or to hear that God loved them, the least we could do was keep walking to intersect those who had been placed in our path.

The walking was difficult, almost impossible at times. But sharing the message of love was pleasurable and enjoyable every single time.

There were, despite the pain, lots of laughs along the way as well. For instance, when we walked through Abingdon, Virginia, we happened across a national women's convention of some type. There were literally hundreds of women, all dressed in red and purple. There were charter buses unloading throngs of women, all adorned in big, floppy hats. We walked down the historic sidewalks, passing log cabins where the likes of Daniel Boone had lived, weaving in and out of the chattering women, choking on their thick perfume and hardly able to contain our giggles. Under normal circumstances, I'm sure this wouldn't have been quite so humorous, but on this day, it was hilarious. Laughter, the Bible says, is good like medicine. This was God's prescription for the day.

Then in Roanoke, Virginia we finally got a chance to go to the mall and get my glasses repaired. The earpiece had broken a few weeks earlier, and they were being held together with tape. The only piece which would fit my glasses was pink. I decided to put fashion and my pride aside and get the pink piece. At least I wouldn't look like a nerd with tape holding my glasses together. Though I have had many different pairs of glasses since then, I decided to keep the ones with the pink earpiece. It still makes me smile when I think about it.

Then, there was the day we went into a bakery to share with the folks behind the counter about our walk and see if we could speak to them about Jesus. We introduced ourselves and so did they. One of the women's names was Dawn. I repeated it, only I said it like the male version of Don. "No," she said emphatically, "it's Dawn." I tried again, but honestly, I didn't hear any difference between my Don and her Dawn. She did. "No, not Don…Dawn." I swear, even when she said them both, side by side, they sounded identical to me. Jane was standing there snickering and thought the whole thing was funny. I thought I must be on Candid Camera or something because I just didn't hear the difference. We must have stood there for five minutes while I tried to adjust my Don to her Dawn. I never did get it right, but we did emerge the bake shop with some of what Dawn called "Preacher cookies." To me, they were no-bake chocolate oatmeal cookies, but I was tired of arguing about names. Besides, it didn't matter what you called them; they were good.

We occasionally did meet fellow travelers. In Virginia, we met Steve Myers, a 48-year-old bicyclist. We had noticed him crawling out from under a bridge a few days earlier on our way out to walk. Steve told us he had ridden from Georgia to Quebec and was now on his way south again. He shared glorious stories of God's faithfulness to him along the way. All Steve owned in this world was his bike, the clothes on his back and the few things in the saddlebags strapped to the sides of his bike. He slept under bridges and ate what he could find. He relied completely on the hand of God to sustain him and he made us a bit ashamed we had ever doubted God's ability to provide for our needs. We gave Steve a McDonald's® gift card and $20. When we met people like Steve, we discovered those were divine appointments too. Sometimes those appointments were so we could encourage others. Many times, they were so others could encourage and challenge us.

It wasn't always the big things or even the serious discussions that blessed us. One afternoon in Virginia we crossed paths with two young boys, maybe twelve or thirteen years old who were out walking. One gave Jane a Jolly Rancher® and the other gave me a gummy worm. It may not sound like much, but at the end of the day when every step takes a real effort, the kindness of two young teenagers who could have been rude or obnoxious meant a lot to us. They said as we were walking away, "You guys are cool."

As we neared the end of our walk, radio and television interviews got more and more frequent. In the beginning, most of the media outlets were skeptical about our chances of finishing. After all, we were two non-athletic adults in their fifties who had never done anything even remotely close to a cross-country walk. By the time we got to Virginia, the story had now become more believable and news outlets were willing to give coverage to our walk. Nearly every day a radio station or newspaper called for a telephone interview. The hits on our website were growing as the media pulled information, stories and pictures from the site to share with their readers or listeners. Some nationally syndicated radio networks like SRN®, Moody Radio® and K-LOVE® had covered the walk across the nation. Even some local radio hosts (one from California) had called every couple of weeks to check on our progress. Television stations now knew our story before we arrived because of the stories their network affiliates had aired in previous cities.

The real challenge was to keep the excitement level up and remember that although we had told the story literally thousands of times across America, for many people this was their first exposure to the Walk to Reclaim America. It didn't really matter how tired we were or how much we hurt. What mattered was we had been entrusted with a precious message of hope. We had been given the opportunity to be spokespeople for a purpose far beyond our own accomplishments. Every interview was another opportunity to talk about His power and His strength which had carried us nearly twenty-five hundred miles across this land. What a platform God had given us from which to speak. Two people like us would never have had the opportunity to speak to tens of thousands of people in person, on the radio, in newspaper articles and on the television were it not for God's call to walk across America. And…so we walked.

Chapter 31

Thinking back on this portion of the walk across America, I am reminded of how historically significant Virginia was to the founding of our country. As we walked through the small towns of rural Virginia, most were filled with buildings present during the late 1700s when the Revolutionary War took place. Historical markers are one of Jane's favorite things and we tried to take time to read as many as possible. Some of the brick buildings were pockmarked where musket balls had hit the walls. Authentic canons sat in front of libraries and empty fields lay fallow where battles had once raged. One theme which consistently reminded us of one of the reasons we were walking was how evident the faith of our young country was. Small, white, clapboard-sided church buildings sat quietly in most every burg and village. Daring sermons proclaiming the virtues of freedom had once emanated from those very pulpits and wafted down the valleys and hollows which surrounded us.

Although there is still a fair amount of debate about the exact theological positions of our founding fathers, one thing seems extremely clear. As you read quotes engraved on plaques and monuments and walk through the hamlets where they lived, it is evident their faith in an Almighty God shaped their calling and strengthened their resolve to see this nation born.

It seemed odd to walk down the streets which two hundred years earlier had been filled with people of hope, vision and faith and see people sitting on those very porches who seemed hopeless, visionless and faithless. What happened in those two centuries to take the spirit of '76 out of the hearts of the American people? Where had faith in God, faith in a government "of the people, by the people and for the people," and faith in the kindness of fellow human beings gone?

Many have attempted to answer those questions and have no doubt filled hundreds of volumes. There is no easy answer. At the risk of great oversimplification, I offer my opinion: Somewhere along the way we have forgotten what Jesus said were the two greatest commandments, the two on which everything else hangs: "Love the Lord your God with all your heart, mind and strength and love your neighbor as yourself."

Our founding fathers did not get it all right. Some of them had some huge blind spots when it came to issues like women's rights and slavery. They did, however, have the foresight to write a document that was durable enough to allow some of those issues to be righted later in our country's history. In addition, they attempted to preserve the priorities of recognizing and crediting the Creator with all that was right about the new nation (loving God) and trying desperately to allow the freedoms necessary for the dignity of people to be protected (loving people). The adhesion to these two principles early on may be partially responsible for America becoming, in just over two centuries, one of the great nations in the history of Western civilization. I would also suggest that the erosion of both of those principles, which had their roots in Jesus' two great commandments, is partially responsible for the hopelessness we observed as we walked down those historic roads. Our nation has become a people who no longer acknowledge God's right to preeminence and who put their own needs and desires above those of others. The degradation of these two spiritual principles has led to a nation full of self-gratifying, self-centered people who brush God and their fellow man aside.

Is it any wonder as we walked through Harrisonburg, Virginia we met people like Doris and Charles sitting outside the *Little Grill*? They were a homeless couple, like so many others we met, with an empty look behind their eyes. Life had worn them down and the flickering flame of hope was all but extinguished. They were clinging to the slight chance Charles would get a job he had applied for on a horse farm, which would provide them with a place to live. We prayed with them and gave them a card with our name and number on it. Charles didn't get the job but over the next several months, Doris called us many times. We sent them boxes of food and personal items to ease their suffering. Our hearts still break when we remember those like Doris and Charles who only desire the bare necessities of life and to be treated with a little dignity.

A few blocks down the street we saw three men sitting on the porch of an old house. As we walked by, we yelled up our usual greeting, "We came to tell you God loves you." Larry, one of the men, called us up on the porch and asked us to pray for him. Jane prayed, and then he asked us for a Bible. Then Dennis, who was holding a beer in his hand, told us he hadn't eaten in four days. He had used his money to buy beer. Jane prayed a powerful prayer asking that alcohol would become repulsive to him since it was obviously ruining his life. When we met our driver a few blocks down the road we sent him back with a Bible for each of them and enough money to take them a good meal. This was only a small gesture and highlighted our larger frustration: We could buy a meal but couldn't do much to change the course of their lives. This we believe to be the responsibility and privilege of the local church. If those who follow Jesus would show the love of Jesus in practical ways to their communities, many like Charles and Doris would be included and cared for rather than excluded and shunned. As we walked, we became more convinced than ever of two things: One, the government does not have the means or the divine call to clothe

the naked, feed the hungry, and restore the disenfranchised. Two, the church has both the means and the call but is sometimes so absorbed in its own agenda and self-promotion that it allows the poor and needy to live within steps of its front door without feeling the slightest conviction to extend the love of Jesus to those in need. With each step we became more and more convinced our journey was awakening a desire to wake the Church to the call to be Jesus to a hurting and desperate world.

Along the way, we met others who shared our convictions. We were also contacted by several people who heard about our walk and wanted us to know they too had felt God's call to do similar things. One such person was Jim Shaner, a man in his sixties who was also walking across America. His method was quite different, but his goal was similar; to enlist people to pray for America. Jim was walking the Discovery Trail, and only walked on weekends and while he was on vacation. We were honored that Jim came and walked with us during one of the most climactic events on the walk…our arrival in New Market, Virginia.

New Market had been on our minds for the last several weeks. This small historic town lay at the last corner we would turn. As we walked through the sleepy town Saturday morning, we met Tim, Sarah and Hallie, a Catholic family from New York City coming out of a restaurant. They were on vacation and told us they prayed for America every day. Then just down the street, we met Susan and her blonde, toddler granddaughter. They were waiting for the little town library to open to return a book. The library was in a building used as a makeshift hospital during the Civil War. Once again, the buildings were scarred with the marks of war and the heaviness of a divided nation still seemed to hang in the air.

We approached the north edge of town and the pall lifted as we saw what we had dreamed of for nearly six months. We turned right on Route 211 with the Shenandoah Mountains directly ahead. Then the most thrilling road sign of the walk thus far: Washington D.C. – 102 miles! There was but one week of walking left ahead. It would be some of the most challenging because of the steep hills and deep valleys immediately in front of us. We also imagined that once we neared Washington, we would find nothing but concrete and heavy traffic, a walker's worst nightmare. The condition of our bodies continued to deteriorate, battered and sore from the constant pounding of our feet against the pavement. My right leg was both numb and in excruciating pain at the same time most all day, every day. Jane's blisters kept coming in the hot, humid weather. We were running on fumes. I was barely walking two miles per hour, and by noon most days, I did not know how I would finish the day. But we knew God had not allowed us to get this close to the end without finishing the walk. And…so we walked.

Chapter 32

The last week seemed like it lasted a month. It rained more than it had during the preceding six months, or at least that's how it felt. Jane fell in the shower, twisting her ankle and hurting her toes. My leg pain had progressed from occasional stabbing pain to a constant icepick sensation with every step. Our driver found the week extremely challenging the closer we got to Washington, meaning it was harder and harder to predict where the van would be for rest, refreshment and for Jane's shoe and sock changes. The frustrations, however, could not change the fact we were only steps from our destination.

The encounters with people had kept us going through many of the most difficult phases of the trip, but as we neared our nation's capital, people got more and more cynical and difficult to talk with about spiritual matters. There were exceptions of course, like Tim and Michelle who owned a bed and breakfast in the mountains of Virginia. They were excited followers of Christ who were thrilled to hear about the walk. Then, there was Elmo, an older African American man whom I teased about being "dancing Elmo." When Jane asked if Jesus was the reason he danced he replied, "Yes ma'am." At a roadside store, Tim and Martha gave us free soft drinks, snacks and freshly picked cherries, but these friendly, encouraging encounters were the exception. Often, the responses were like Phyllis at the Citgo gas station who said she knew as much about God as she cared to know right now. Some responded, "not interested" or got away from us as quickly as possible, and most were visibly hostile toward anything they perceived as religious. We got more respect from those who told us they were Hindu and Muslim than from what we might consider normal, white (Christian) Americans. The melting pot phenomenon became more and more apparent as we neared D.C. Recent immigrants who spoke broken English and were first-generation Americans became a predominant percentage of the population. We found ourselves adapting our message to our surroundings and changing the language a bit in order to speak more effectively of our Savior's love. That Story now had to be contextualized to speak to those who had not been raised in the Bible belt or in a Sunday school classroom. It's hard to explain, but the story of the walk broke down barriers with those of other religions. They were simply amazed anyone could be so affected by their faith they would walk across America. We believe during those difficult final days of the walk many spiritual seeds were planted in the hearts of those seeking the truth.

The combination of a deep sense of calling, physical pain, emotional and mental exhaustion, and a sense of fulfillment made every event more intense than it normally would have been. One such occasion was walking through the Civil War battlefields of Manassas, Virginia. Long before the walk, I had envisioned us stopping each day for lunch under a tree, spreading out a blanket and resting for an hour or so. On Wednesday of the last week of the walk, we stopped for lunch in the middle of the Manassas battlefield, spread out a blanket under a tree and for the first time, enjoyed the restful lunch I'd been dreaming about all those months.

As we sat there that hot, summer afternoon, our hearts were broken and we both shed tears as we imagined we could be sitting in the very spot where a soldier lost his life for something he believed in. The enormous weight of all those emotions was almost more than we could endure. Looking back on it now, I suppose we may have been close to an emotional break. We were now within hours of reaching our goal. Our life had revolved around the walk for more than a year and a half. We had no plans beyond July 4th, 2006. The walk had changed us in ways that prohibited us from ever going back to life as usual. Sitting on the battlefield that day brought all those thoughts into a frightening focus.

As our lunch break ended and we gathered up our belongings, we knew only one thing: Although we had no idea what the future held, we did know what must be done in the next couple of days. We must walk through the remaining battlefields, both literal and figurative, and finish the course. And…so we walked.

Chapter 33

By the afternoon of Friday, June 30th, we had walked to the edge of Arlington Memorial Cemetery. We had made it to within a few blocks of Washington D.C. with three days to spare. Our family, friends, pastor and several of our drivers would be there to join us as we walked across the bridge into Washington on July 4th. We had three days to rest!

As those who came to celebrate with us began to trickle into the hotel which would serve as our headquarters for the last few days, every arrival triggered floods of emotions. When drivers arrived, like Ron and Betty Teed, we remembered the Petrified Forest and Painted Desert and how faithful they had been to obey the call of God to come to drive for two people they had never met before. When our pastor, Mark Garrett arrived, I remembered the first day I had gone to his office to tell him about our call to walk across America. He never doubted the call although he may have doubted my sanity. When our daughters arrived, it was unbelievable. We hadn't seen Rebekah since my accident in April in Russellville, Arkansas. When Shoshannah arrived, she had been in China for most of the last year and during all of the walk. Perhaps the most significant arrival was that of my parents, Ruth and JC McKinney. They had endured a very difficult six months, and my mom's health had been deteriorating dramatically. She arrived in a wheelchair, but with a smile on her face. Mom and Dad had seen me do a lot of crazy things in my life. They knew I was a dreamer and a non-conformist, but if it had to do with Jesus, they never did anything but support me. My sisters, brother-in-law, aunts, other drivers and friends rounded out the support team who would join us as we took the last few steps.

The night before the final steps was a busy one. We had arranged to gather all our friends and family together for a celebration banquet at Olive Garden in Falls Church, Virginia. We continued doing what we had done for the last six months; we shared Jesus with everyone we met. Our servers. Safri, a Muslim and Antonio, a Catholic got to hear our story as we shared at the banquet. Afterward, we made sure we had an opportunity to personally tell them about our wonderful Savior. It was a beautiful way to end the evening and the final hours of the walk.

The morning of July 4th came after a restless night. We felt like children on Christmas Eve multiplied by ten. Jane and I got up early and took a cab to where we would begin walking through Arlington. The only thing left was to walk through the cemetery and to the Virginia side of the bridge leading into Washington where we would meet all the others. We entered the upper side of the cemetery near the Iwo Jima Monument. It was the perfect beginning to the last day of the walk. There, gathered around the monument, was the Marine Band playing hymns. Tears welled up in our eyes as we felt as though God had opened heaven and His voice was confirming all that had been accomplished, saying "These are my children in whom I am well pleased." We could hear the music as we continued down through the grave sites of those who had given their lives in service to our country. We had not planned to walk through the cemetery, but it was obviously orchestrated by our God. It was one final divine appointment.

We were feeling our way toward the bridge but couldn't seem to find our way. The rock walls were too high to scale, and we were beginning to wonder how we would get out. We were running close on time and we knew our group of thirty or so friends and family would be anxious if we didn't arrive soon. Finally, we found a rock wall that was short enough to get over and we crossed the busy boulevard and arrived at the entrance to the bridge where we found one last obstacle we had never imagined.

"BRIDGE CLOSED!" Never in a million years could we have planned on this last irritation. There had been an anonymous threat to blow up the bridge and given the post-9/11 atmosphere in the nation's capital, every threat was taken seriously. We begged and pleaded, even told the people we'd cross at our own risk, but it became apparent rather quickly we weren't crossing the bridge until the authorities reopened it.

This was not only inconvenient but a big logistical problem as well. Faith and Action Ministries in Washington D.C. had been instrumental in scheduling the last day of activities, including prayers as we entered the Capitol and a closing rally and prayer meeting on the steps of the Supreme Court. The permit had been issued for a specific time and we could not miss the deadline. Shortly after arriving at the bridge, a reporter from the Washington Post approached us. The delay gave us time to give a lengthy interview about the walk to one the nation's leading newspapers, an opportunity which we may have missed had the bridge been open when we first arrived. After over an hour of waiting the bridge finally opened. Jane and I walked across into Washington D.C. holding hands. In the walk of nearly twenty-eight hundred miles, we rarely walked side by side. Most often she led the way and I followed. I joked all across America that my scenery never changed, I was always looking at the same thing. But today we walked together, flanked by our friends and family.

When we got to the other side of the bridge, we knelt on a grassy spot beside the Lincoln Memorial and prayed. There are no words to describe the flood of emotions which washed over us in those moments. There we were with a group of people who had sacrificed, prayed, believed, and supported us in what seemed like an impossible task. They had called us, prayed with us over the phone, helped raise much-needed financial support and defended the word we felt God had spoken to us to those who doubted. There was my mom sitting in a wheelchair with my dad kneeling beside her. I knew she had shed many tears for me over the course of my fifty years, and I was here in large part due to the consistency and intensity of those prayers. There was our pastor who had taken me to Washington in September of 2005 to make our plans to walk across America and finish with a rally on the Supreme Court steps. He had flown to Los Angeles to help us kick off the walk, come to Oklahoma City for the halfway rally, and had providentially been in the Little Rock area when I burned myself and was taken to the Burn Center. There were drivers kneeling on the grass whose own lives had been transformed by being a part of the walk. And then there was my sweetheart and closest friend of over thirty years kneeling beside me, holding my hands, celebrating the most unbelievable accomplishment two people could ever share together.

We had walked across America…every day…every step…together. There was not another person in the world who would have believed me at the depth my wife did when I said, "God wants us to walk across America." There was not another human being who would have endured the pain and suffering she did in order to fulfill her promise and commitment to me and to God. There was not another person alive who would have put up with my irritability, my doubt, and my own physical inability the way she did. She set the pace, physically and spiritually, for the walk across America. I have no problem admitting that had it not been for her commitment and courage, I would never have completed the journey. She never signed up for this crazy life, but she has unwaveringly stood by my side in every call I have received from God. As I heard the last "amen" of the prayer, I realized it was almost over. We had accomplished what God had asked of us except for one thing. The instructions were clear: We were to end the walk with a rally, speech and prayer on the Supreme Court steps. Rob had arranged for two cabs to pick us up and take a small group of us, including my parents, to the Supreme Court. The rest of the group would take the subway. We arrived just in time for the permit to be honored and I stood to give my speech. Although public speaking rarely made me nervous, this time was different. This was the steps of the Supreme Court of the United States of America. We were surrounded by the media, friends, family and tourists who had stopped to watch. As I began to speak, the words each seemed to form a lump in my throat:

"Six months, 2770 miles, 20 pairs of shoes, and over 10 million steps ago, Jane and I set out from Santa Monica Pier in Los Angeles, California with the intention of walking across America. I am overjoyed to report to you today that we these last few steps we have just taken, we have completed that task. When we took those first steps on Sunday morning, January 1st, we could not have imagined all that lay ahead."

I thought of all the unexpected trials, tragedies and triumphs. The faces of those we had met flashed through my mind in an instant. The emotion was almost overwhelming. Had I not been able to see Jane's reassuring smile in my peripheral vision, I probably could not have finished. I continued reading the speech through teary eyes until I got to the last two sentences:

"The Walk To Reclaim America has changed us forever. We have come to understand that if we can help to change one life at a time, one step at a time, that we have a chance to change America."

After the speech, Jane and I climbed the first set of steps to the Supreme Court and there joined hands and bowed our heads for the final prayer of the Walk to Reclaim America. We had offered thousands of prayers from one side of our country to another. Never had we prayed so much or with such earnestness for any one thing. We had not prayed for one political party or viewpoint. We had not prayed against any group of people. We had not prayed conservative or liberal prayers. We had simply prayed our nation would once again become a nation which recognized and relied on God and which reflected His nature by caring for those in need. That was our first prayer and our last. We had heard God's call to walk and pray…to walk and share…to walk one step at a time from one side of the nation to the other. And…so we walked.

Chapter 34

One of the questions Jane and I are asked most is about how the walk changed us. The answer could fill another book and perhaps one day it will. One of the reasons I'm glad it has taken me several years to write this book is that time has revealed the deep and meaningful ways in which our lives have been transformed. I'm certain we could not have seen that just a few weeks or months after the walk. To fully understand how our lives have changed, you must remember what we saw as we crossed our country. We have tried to give you a glimpse into our experiences but nothing except a walk of your own could ever give you a true perspective.

First, we got to see the immensity of this nation in a way few people do. Driving across America gives you a kind of Cliff notes version of America. What you see driving at Interstate speed is meaningful, but a shallow experience compared to walking. When you touch America the way we did, one step at a time, you get connected to it in an unfathomable way. From that experience, we learned to appreciate the vastness of this land. There are places where you can literally walk for days and never see another human being. God has blessed us with a land that is the most strikingly beautiful, abundantly filled with natural resources, and decorated with the most interesting and diverse wildlife one could imagine. This land is a divine gift that we under-appreciate and take for granted.

Second, we had the privilege of meeting thousands of people. We met people from every kind of background, of every color, nationality and religion, and with as many stories to tell as we cared to listen to. We walked through Native American reservations, inter-city slums, gay communities, past redneck cabins, and what some people might classify as dangerous and unsafe neighborhoods. We met mentally and emotionally ill people. We met some confused people. We even met a few rude people. But after meeting all those folks, many of whom were kind and gracious, we did not meet one person who did not need the gracious gift of forgiveness which comes through accepting Jesus Christ. Each day we were reminded that every person, no matter who they are, needs Jesus.

Third, we confirmed something we already knew by theory but not by experience. We saw firsthand what people really need is to experience God's love as demonstrated through His children. Not the church, not religion, not hypocrisy, not a judgmental attitude, but real honest-to-goodness love which emanates from a real relationship with God. Most people just want to feel loved, not for what they can be used for, but for who they are. Sometimes, it just meant giving someone a smile or a hug who hadn't received one in a long time. Sometimes it meant giving someone a five-dollar McDonald's® card to buy a meal. Sometimes it just meant taking the time to talk to someone and listen to their story. People are drawn to genuine love, and that kind of love comes from God. We came to understand that loving people in practical ways isn't a substitute for the gospel. Instead, it opens the door for gospel conversations in which the most basic need of that person can be discussed, their need for a Savior.

The fourth and perhaps most life-changing lesson we learned is that one person really can make a difference. We found joy is contagious, hope is viral, smiles are irresistible, and a kind word can work miracles. One person can brighten a room or a street corner. If you think one person can't make a difference, you're wrong.

As I said, there are hundreds of lessons we learned, but those four may be the most important. We learned our walk didn't end in Washington D.C. It only started there. When we left the steps of the Supreme Court, we became ambassadors called to continue the journey and share what we learned with others. We may never walk across America again, but we can walk where God leads us and share what He's taught us. Our daily walk is different now than it was for those six months. These days we walk in the grocery store, at the gas station, and around the local parks. But we are still looking for and finding those divine appointments to share the glorious, good news of the gospel. And…so we walk.

One Final Thought and Challenge

One of the most poignant lessons of the walk was not really driven home until after the walk's conclusion. A week or two after we returned home, we spoke at Legacy Christian Church in Harrison, Ohio, one of the main supporters of The Walk To Reclaim America. Pastor Bill McConnel had graciously given us the entire service to share about our adventure.

One of the last stories we shared was about Rick, the Navajo in Winslow, Arizona for whom I had purchased lunch. I shared about the waitress wanting to give Rick "to-go" containers for his meal. At the end of the service, as we were beginning to celebrate communion together, one of the elders began to pray. Through tears and pauses to try to regain her composure she prayed, "Lord, thank you that at Your table there are no "to-go" containers. Thank you that everyone is welcome at Your table."

After several years of reflection on the walk across America, perhaps this is still the penetrating truth we learned. It has affected the way we see people, the way we treat people and most of all, the way we minister to people. Never again would we see "us" and "them." Never again would there be anyone too dirty, too tattooed, too different, too smelly or too disabled to invite to His table. Their place at the table was every bit as wide as ours and their names have been written on the placards welcoming them to the Lord's place of mercy just like ours have been.

Our last question for our readers is this: Is there room at the table you're sitting at for those who are not like you? Because if there's not, you may not be sitting at the Lord's Table. You too may need to walk…like we had to walk…from where you are to where He is.

Appendix One

Now that you've read our story, you can appreciate the questions and answers that are most frequently asked when we share about our journey. A few of these facts were contained within the story itself, but just in case you didn't catch them, here they are.

How many pairs of shoes did you wear out?

Jane and I started the walk with about 8 pairs each, one of which was a very specialized, high-quality trail shoe. We tried many shoe brands and styles in the year before the walk as we trained. We had our feet analyzed by shoe experts so we could compensate for our imperfect stride. The shoes were numbered and rotated at least twice a day. Jane had to switch more often because of the moisture build-up inside her shoes, but generally, we wore pairs #1 and #2 on Monday, #3 and #4 on Tuesday, and so on. Before we left California, we bought additional pairs so in theory at least, we would only need to wear a pair of shoes once per week. By the end of the walk, we had completely worn out 20 pairs of shoes. The only shoes we can still wear from the walk are the trail shoes. One other thing about walking twenty miles per day: Your shoe size increases because of swelling. Most of our shoes were 1 to 2 sizes larger than we would normally wear. Several months after the walk, my shoe size returned to within a half-size of normal. Jane's feet never returned to her petite size 5. She now wears size 6 – 6 1/2. The incredible punishment of putting your body weight down on your feet about 5 million times, causes your feet to spread out and change shape. I'm sure in Jane's case, the scar tissue from the constant blisters also affected the size of her feet. Another very disappointing fact for me was that I lost about one-and-a-half- inches of height over the six months.

How fast did you walk?

Our normal pace was 3 miles per hour. However, we did not average that on most days. Stopping to talk with people, shoe and sock changes, lunch breaks and other issues delayed us. We experimented with different paces during the year of training and found this pace to be most comfortable for both of us. We could walk faster but found it took a higher toll on our bodies. We could have gone slower and near the end of the walk, my pace had slowed substantially because of my leg injury. To walk 20-21 miles per day at 3 miles per hour means you're walking seven hours. The truth was, including driving back and forth to the starting point and camp each day, stops, conversations, lunch, etc. we were away from camp an average of 10-11 hours per day.

How much weight did you lose?

Surprisingly from the starting date to the end date, we gained weight. We lost a significant amount of weight the year we trained. We lost a few pounds the first few weeks but then remained steady and were a few pounds heavier by July 4th. The body is a miraculous thing. It seemed to adjust to the amount of exercise we were doing. We thought we'd lose lots of weight but just didn't. Our calorie intake was higher during the walk, ingesting as much protein as possible. The great thing about walking 20 miles per day is that you can eat just about anything you want and not gain too much weight!

Where did you sleep and how did you get to and from your route each day?

Because we were on the road full-time for a few years before the walk, we owned an older motorhome. In theory, this was the way it worked. We planned on walking 100-120 miles per week on average. We would find a campground as close to the middle of the next week's walk as possible on Saturdays after we were finished for the week. On Monday we would leave the motor home parked at the campground and the drivers would take us backward 60 miles or so to the beginning point of the day. They stayed with us throughout the day (within walkie-talkie range) with food, water and medical supplies. At the end of the day, they would take us back to camp, which by then was only 40 miles away. We drove a stake in the ground at night, so we'd know where to start in the morning. We'd go back to the camp, shower, eat, take care of aching muscles and blistered feet and try to be in bed by 8 or 9 p.m. The next morning they'd drive us 40 miles back to the starting point. That's how it worked across the country. Then on Saturday when we finished walking for the week, we'd hook up the van behind the motor home and drive 120 miles down the road to the next campground.

What were the hottest and coldest temperatures when you were walking?

The coldest morning was in Gallup, New Mexico at 5 degrees above zero. The wind made it feel much colder. There were many days when the temperatures were near or slightly above 100 degrees. On those days, the heat index was substantially higher. The only place there was snow on the ground was at the Oklahoma/Texas state line, but it melted quickly. The hardest snowstorm was in Clines Corner, New Mexico although the pavement was warm, and it didn't accumulate. However, we did walk the entire day on the Interstate which was scary. The worst rainstorms and lightning were near Jackson, Tennessee. In Oklahoma, we walked through several tornado warnings and were close enough to see a funnel cloud one day.

Did you both walk every step, or did you tag-team?

We both walked every step. We felt there was a spiritual principle involved. It would have been much easier to walk it tag-team style alternating miles or hours, but we didn't. Most of the time it was just Jane and me. We did have friends and family who walked a few miles here and there, perhaps a total of 60 or 70 miles, but the other 2700 or so was just us.

Do you keep in touch with people from the walk?

We still communicate with many people who drove and supported the walk. Some are still dear friends in whom we have great spiritual confidence. These are people who believed in this extraordinary call, gave of themselves sacrificially in many ways and encouraged us when it was not easy to do so.

Many of the people described in this book have passed away since the walk. Many have moved, and we've lost track of them. We kept the toll-free number for about a year after the walk and got calls on a regular basis from people whom we gave cards to along the way for as long as the number was in service.

One friend that we met on the walk, Evelyn Lookebill has become a very dear friend. She lives in Muldrow, OK and we communicate regularly. We had the privilege of meeting her for lunch lately, 14 years after we met.

Would you do it again?

Honestly, under the same circumstances, I would. It was the hardest six months of our lives in practically every way, but it was also the greatest. The lessons we learned, the faith that developed and the people we met made all the expense, physical pain and time away from family worth it. I have often contemplated a walk from the tip of Southern Texas to the Canadian border, but the look I get from Jane every time I mention it tells me I may have to do it alone. Seriously, if we both felt as led to do it as we did in 2005 -2006 then yes, even knowing all we know now, and even being much older, we'd do it again, without question.

Jane and I have talked many times about how we wish our faith and trust in God was as great now as it was then. The truth is, that kind of faith and trust usually come when you have gone beyond your own limits and must trust in God. Sadly, most of us chose not to put ourselves in that position very often, if ever.

What are you doing now?

For about a year after the walk, we continued to travel and speak about our journey. In 2007, we made the decision to come off the road and re-enter the pastorate. Since then, I have had the wonderful privilege of leading churches to embrace the call of ministering to the people in their communities. We have modeled what we learned on the walk by beginning ministries to the homeless, working with the residents of rescue missions, integrating recently released prisoners into churches, and reaching into low-income neighborhoods with the tangible love of Jesus. Our lives were forever changed by the walk across America and our ministry has been deeply affected by those steps we took. We have never again been able to look at people in the same way or with the same attitudes. We have never again been able to settle for living the same old way. Currently, (2023) God has opened the door for me to do something I've dreamed of all my life. I am teaching at a university. The opportunity to share a lifetime of our experiences, including the walk across America, is a blessing. In addition, Jane teaches high school students each day and gets opportunities to share the love of Jesus with them. It appears God isn't quite done with us yet.

Thank God, He changed us with every step we took…and so, we walked.

If you've enjoyed the book and it has been meaningful to you, we ask that you please go to Amazon and leave a rating and review on our book's page. Thank you so much.

Printed in Great Britain
by Amazon